SAM BAILEY

DARING TO DREAM

SAM BAILEY

DARING TO DREAM

BLINK
bringing you closer

Published by Blink Publishing
Deepdene Lodge
Deepdene Avenue
Dorking RH5 4AT, UK

www.blinkpublishing.co.uk

facebook.com/blinkpublishing
twitter.com/blinkpublishing

978-1-905825-93-6

A CIP catalogue of this book is available from the British Library.

Design by www.envydesign.co.uk

Printed and bound by Clays Ltd, St Ives Plc

3 5 7 9 10 8 6 4 2

Papers used by Blink Publishing are natural, recyclable products made from wood grown in sustainable forests. The manufacturing processes conform to the environmental regulations of the country of origin.

Every reasonable effort has been made to trace copyright holders of material reproduced in this book, but if any have been inadvertently overlooked the publishers would be glad to hear from them.

Blink Publishing is an imprint of the Bonnier Publishing Group
www.bonnierpublishing.co.uk

CONTENTS

ACKNOWLEDGEMENTS

Special thanks to my mum Jackie, Craig's mum and dad Sally and Eddie, and Craig's brothers and their wives, Gavin and Sarah and Greg and Laura. They've been there for us throughout everything and Craig and I are incredibly grateful.

I also want to thank Sharon Osbourne because she's a massive inspiration to me and I honestly don't think I would have got as far if I didn't have her as a mentor. Michael Bolton was also my secret mentor during the show and he's like a spiritual guru to me. He's given me a shoulder to cry on and been on the phone to me from LA whenever I've needed him.

My hometown of Leicester has also been incredible. People have been so lovely and Leicester City Football Club have welcomed me with open arms. It's such a pleasure and an honour to be a part of such a great institution.

I also want to give a special mention to a couple called Chris and Nigel Pitchfork who have followed my singing career for many years and have been a great support to me.

I want to thank *The X Factor* for giving me such an incredible opportunity and allowing me not just to change my life for the better, but also the lives of those closest to me. And, of course, my fans who have made all this possible: your dedication amazes me and you always know how to put a smile on my face.

Finally I want to thank my husband Craig and my kids Brooke, Tommy and Miley. None of this would have been possible without their incredible love and support. They are my absolute world.

FOREWORD
BY
SHARON OSBOURNE

'Sam.I.am'… that's what I called you from the very start. From the moment you walked into the first audition room, stood in front of all of us and announced you were a prison officer, you had my attention. I asked you if your dream was to sing and you said 'yes' and then you completely stole my heart with your rendition of 'Listen' by Beyoncé. As you left that first audition I turned to the other judges and said 'That's our winner' and they all agreed with me.

Sam, your strength, your voice and your transformation as the weeks went by was something to behold and was an honour for me to be a part of. Keep on living the dream. God bless, loves ya.

Mrs O

PROLOGUE

I'm standing on stage in front of 10,000 screaming people and it feels like a million lights are pointing right at me. The sound of an incredibly loud heartbeat is pulsating around me and everything feels like it's moving in slow motion. Suddenly Dermot O'Leary says something and I look to my left to see Sharon Osbourne collapsing onto the floor in tears. It takes a few seconds for the words to sink in but then it hits me. I've just won *The X Factor*.

CHAPTER 1

BABY LOVE

I came into the world on 29th June 1977 at Stone Park Maternity Hospital in Beckenham, south-east London. Because I had two older brothers, Danny and Charlie, my parents were expecting another boy to come along. So when I popped out my dad had to go and buy me a dress straight-away. They only had my brothers' hand-me-downs and so Dad got me this tiny pink fluffy thing that I've still got in a box in my loft.

Mum says I was named after my uncle Sammy on her side, but my dad always said I was named after Samantha Stephens from the TV show *Bewitched* because he had a crush on her. That would be a very 'my dad' thing to do.

Mum said that dad treated me very differently to my brothers from the word go because he thought I was so much more delicate than they were as babies. Every time he heard a murmur from my cot he'd run over and say to my mum, 'What's wrong with her?' He was always panicking that I was going to get ill. Mum said he'd sit there and watch over me for hours and hours sometimes.

When I was first born we lived in a maisonette in Anerley Vale, Crystal Palace. With a new arrival and my brothers growing at a rapid rate we soon ran out of space, so my parents decided to move house, to Walnuts Road in Orpington, Kent. My first *real* memories are of living in that house. It was a council house that had the old green metal council fencing outside. When I was about three I used to play in the front garden with our big Afghan hound, Jaffa, and I remember it really clearly. She was so big she seemed more like a horse than a dog and of course I was always trying to climb up on her. I've always thought Jaffa was the reason my mum and dad didn't have any more kids after me. She used to sleep in between them every night so there was no chance of them having any kind of hanky-panky!

One day a family knocked on our door and asked my mum if they could borrow our dog to breed her. Mum says now that they seemed really shifty, and of course she wasn't about to let some total strangers walk off with our dog, so she told them where to go. A couple of weeks later two of the men came back while I was toddling around with Jaffa in the garden, picked her up and took her away right in front of my eyes. Of course I didn't really understand what was going on, but I started screaming and ran inside to Mum.

That was the last time we ever saw Jaffa; she was found in a field some months later. Terribly, she'd been shot dead. We can only assume that the people who took her bred her and then decided they didn't need her any more. It's not the nicest memory to have and I'm still shocked people that horrible exist in the world.

Other early – and happier – memories I have are of walking across a footbridge to get to the Walnut Centre, which was my nursery. I always used to get really excited about going because they had such amazing toys. Mum worked for a company called Specac, which had a big factory nearby, and every day she'd drop me off and pick me up again. My dad was working as a painter and decorator at the time, and he was also a musician, so both of them were grafters.

When I was about six we moved again, this time to Lockesley Drive in St Mary Cray, Kent, and I had to start at a big new school called St Philomena's. I'd missed the first year, so when I joined I didn't know anyone and my classmates had already made friends and formed groups. A girl called Vicky Lovesey and I became friends and she's still a friend of mine now. But sadly I wasn't exactly inundated with friendship requests in my first year at school.

Back then I had a real problem with wetting myself. And not just wetting the bed – it could happen anytime. As a result I had to wear nappies to school just in case I had an accident (which was a frequent occurrence), so needless to say that instantly made me a target for bullies. I got called names and laughed at, and I felt really ostracised. It was so horrible: I used to ask if I could stay in the classroom and write lines every break time just so I didn't have to hang out with the other kids. The headmistress, Mrs Shelley-Pierce, was a lovely woman and I think she felt a bit sorry for me because at lunchtime she'd let me go into her office and sharpen pencils to save me from being hassled in the playground.

Vicky became my only friend and I used to get a lift to school with her and her mum every morning. We'd get dropped at the end of a lane and then walk the rest of the way, but as soon as we got into the school grounds she would ignore me. One day she turned to me, pointed to the end of the lane and said, 'We're only friends to here.' She didn't want to be seen with me in case the other kids turned on her too. We were only young and she probably doesn't even remember it, and I am over it now – honestly! I know what children are like now I've got my own. They can be cruel and they don't understand how much it affects someone when you pick on them. I totally forgive everyone who was unkind to me when I was younger because I had a problem. I *was* smelly, so I do understand why the other kids didn't want to hang out with me. I probably would have avoided me too.

My parents tried *everything* to stop me wetting myself. I went to see a psychiatrist and all sorts. I even had a star chart where I'd get rewarded if I went an entire day without weeing myself, which was rare. I went to see one doctor who gave me a metal sheet to put on my bed (yes, *really*). The idea was that every time I wet the bed an alarm would go off. It sounded like a loud bell and so woke up the whole house. My mum would come running in and say, 'Quick, you need to go to the toilet!' But by then I'd already gone, so I never really understood the point of it. Maybe it was to subconsciously shame me into not doing it any more? Well, it didn't bloody work. It must have been incredibly frustrating for my parents and I used to get so embarrassed.

When I got to the age of eight I started trying to fit in at school by playing the class clown. One day I went to the toilet – I was the only person who was allowed to go whenever they wanted, for obvious reasons – and I decided to have a bit of a laugh and impress my classmates. There was a high window that looked onto my class, so I climbed up to it by clambering on the coat hooks and putting my foot into the pocket of this boy called Gerald's duffle coat to keep me steady. I started to do a 'V' sign at the window but then I heard this ripping sound and realised I'd ripped Gerald's pocket quite badly. I went back to the classroom and didn't say a word, but when the teacher found out about the damage she demanded someone own up to it. I kept quiet and the next thing I knew our teacher had called the police in. Only of course it was someone's dad who happened to be a police officer. He carried out an 'investigation', which eventually led back to me and I had to own up. Gerald's mum came round to my house clutching the coat and made my parents pay for it. I felt awful and I remember thinking, 'Look where trying to be funny and fit in has got you.'

Something else that got me into trouble at school was my dad's band. We all had to write an English essay about our family, and then go up to the front of the class and read them out. Our teacher didn't check them first, so I announced to the entire class that my dad was the drummer in a band called *Sex With Strangers*, obviously having no idea what it actually meant. I thought my teacher was going to have a heart attack and he quickly sent a letter home to my parents – but my dad found it hilarious!

The one thing that saved me at school was sport. I became really good at football and cross-country running because it gave me a way to escape. Until then I'd been really lazy and I was still being wheeled around in one of those really old-fashioned deckchair pushchairs because I refused to walk anywhere. Yes, even at the age of eight. Sport gave me purpose and focus and, because I was good at it, a bit more confidence; it was also a relief for my mum who was sick of wheeling me around in that pushchair!

Cross-country was a real release because it meant that I could be totally on my own and think. I lived with constant noise around me at home – either my dad would be playing loud music or my brothers would be kicking the 'living daylights' out of each other – so that was the one time I could be away from everything. It was my only way of experiencing true silence.

I joined the Brownies for a while, but we were all told to write a pretend pen pal letter to someone else in the group and I didn't realise the Brownie leaders were going to read them, so I put loads of swear words in mine. I wasn't exactly upset when they said I couldn't go back. I didn't like having to wear a skirt and a stupid sash anyway. I was never going to be the girl who was good at gymnastics, either. I was far from graceful, but if you gave me a football I could play for hours. There was a lad on my football team back then called Michael Delaney, who has got his own football academy now. He's taught people like Cristiano Ronaldo and David Beckham how to do incredible tricks for TV adverts. He choreographs the routines and he's an amazing footballer. I used to watch what he did and copy him, and I picked up a lot of good skills even at that age.

I think mum was keen to try and stop me from being permanently muddy, so she signed me up for dance classes. But obviously me wearing a leotard and tights with my toilet issue wasn't the best idea in the world. I was still really suffering and if I had an incident there was no hiding it. I used to go to classes on Orpington High Street and it was right near where my mum had started working in a greasy spoon called The Golden Egg. I'd go into the cafe after class and have egg and chips and I loved it. It was always a real treat for me, and it almost made going to dance classes worth it.

I was a really fussy eater when I was young, and to a certain extent I still am now. At dinner times I always used to make sure I had this giant plastic cup with a lid that I'd got from a theme park. I'd drink all of my drink really quickly and then hide any food I didn't like inside it. As soon as we were allowed down from the table I'd go out into the garden and feed it all to our neighbours' Alsatian, Sheba. If it looked like I'd finished all of my mains, I could have a mousse or a donut for pudding, which were my favourites. I only really liked sweet things and I didn't eat much, so I was a tiny child, very slim and small for my age. I was also quite headstrong.

When I was six I had a huge argument with my mum and told her I was leaving home. She packed me a bag and waved me off, and to test me she let me walk all the way up the road. When I got to the top I sat there for about 20 minutes to make her think I'd really gone. She could still see me from the upstairs window so she let me stew, and in the end I stormed back home, said, 'I've got to stay now, I've forgotten something', and stomped up to my room. I had a really determined nature and I hated people getting the better of me.

Mum always knew how to play me but I got away with murder with my dad. I was the apple of his eye. He had these amazing mahogany speakers in our living room that he was so proud of and there was always music blaring out of them. It was usually a band called Budgie, who my dad knew, or Fleetwood Mac or Queen. Even now if I hear any of the songs that were played back then I don't just hear the song. I hear people shouting over the top of it and my dad talking and laughing and it takes me straight back to my front room filled with about 20 of my parents' friends.

One day my brothers were winding me up as usual and I was holding a ginger nut biscuit, which I threw at Danny. He dodged out of the way and it hit one of the speakers and dented it. We all gasped and when my dad came running in, even though it was my fault, it was my brothers who got the telling off because they'd been goading me. I could do no wrong as far as he was concerned.

Dad's love of music definitely rubbed off on me, although I have to shamefully admit that the first song I ever bought was 'We All stand Together' by Paul McCartney and the Frog Chorus. My brothers and I went into town with our pocket money one Saturday and Charlie bought Stevie Wonder's 'I Just Called To Say I Love You' and Danny bought 'When The Going Gets Tough' by Billy Ocean. We used to play those three songs over and over again in my brothers' bedroom. My single wasn't allowed to be played as much because the boys found it annoying, and I remember being so upset when I found a couple of giant scratches on it, which I'm pretty sure were done on purpose.

I adored my family but I did used to feel quite lonely as a child due to my lack of friends. I used to buy sweets on the way to school just so I could give them out to everyone that was unkind to me in the hope they might like me. I used to get invited to a lot of kids' parties, but only because the mums used to invite every child in my class. I never wanted to go because I knew the birthday girl or boy probably didn't want me there, but my mum insisted on sending me off in these really awful girlie dresses. She'd come and pick me up and I'd be up a tree with the lads throwing conkers at the girls. Maybe it wasn't that much of a surprise that the girls didn't warm to me?

My brothers' mates were always coming round, so I guess I got used to hanging out with lots of lads really early on, and I think that really shaped me. I was much more comfortable around boys than girls because at least they were upfront about everything and spoke their minds. The girls at school would be nice to my face and then laugh at me behind my back, and I found that so much more upsetting than someone calling me a stupid name.

Danny's best mate was a guy called Stephen Cameron, who was lovely. He was one of the few lads who was always friendly and made time for me when we were growing up. Sadly, many years later, when he was 21, he was involved in a high-profile road rage incident, which resulted in him being murdered by a guy called Kenneth Noye. I remember it being all over the news at the time and it seems so surreal to think that was the same little boy who used to come round to ours all the time for dinner.

When I got a bit older my brothers turned into horrible pre-teens who no longer thought their little sister was cute and so started calling me Piss Flaps due to my little 'problem'. But to be fair, I was just as horrible to them. My brother Charlie, who is four years older than me, had really bad acne so we all used to call him Pizza Face, and Danny, who is three years older, had one ear that stuck out so we'd nicknamed him Wingnut. We weren't shy about taking the mickey out of each other in our house.

I did as much sport as I could when I was at school because it meant spending fewer playtimes with the bullies. One day I got a searing pain in my right foot. Mum took me to the doctors but they couldn't find anything wrong. I couldn't put my heel to the floor so they sent me home with some crutches and I was hopping around school on them all of the next week. I was in agony, so eventually my doctor referred me to a specialist and they decided to operate. When I came round after the operation the doctor told my mum and I that in his 30 years of being a doctor he'd never seen as much poison in someone's foot. They had to drain it all out and if they hadn't operated when they did I could have lost part of my leg. He thought I must have trodden on something that led to it becoming badly infected, so I had a very lucky escape.

I was in hospital for a week and I was going round the children's ward helping the nurses cheer up the other kids. They even got me a little nurse outfit and that was such a boost to me because I finally felt accepted after all that time feeling like an outcast. My classmates also sent get-well presents in for me. I used to collect those little rubbers that you put on top of your pencil and every single one of my classmates brought one in for me and put it in a box with a card. There were ones shaped like animals and ones that smelt of strawberries and all sorts. I was so excited because I thought it meant the other children in my class cared about me. Sadly, as soon as I went back to school it was back to being the way it had always been. I tried to join in a game of Kiss Chase on the first day (well, Hobble Chase in my case) and all the boys ran away from me shouting 'Eurgh!' But that didn't stop me *fancying* boys.

My first ever childhood crush was on a boy called Ben Disdin, who I thought was amazing. To me he looked like a model, but he wasn't interested in me. I don't think he was interested in any girls at that point; he preferred playing British Bulldog. My first kiss was with a boy called Daniel Cappuccio underneath a coat in the school playground. He had dark hair and glasses and his uncle was Tony Cascarino, who used to play for Millwall, so I felt like I'd kissed a celebrity. I was only nine and it was a very innocent peck, but I was so happy that someone wanted to come within ten yards of me after years of being either ignored or made fun of by all of the boys.

I loved our house in Loxley Drive but when I was 11 we got offered the chance to exchange it for a four-bedroom place on the North Cray estate in Sidcup. It meant we would have a lot more room but I was gutted to leave Walnuts Road. My poor mum had to take me on two buses to school every day and then go to work at Specac. She had three jobs at that time: one in the factory, one in the greasy spoon, and she also worked part time as a cleaner. I've always been a hard worker and I think I get that from her because she literally never stopped.

I was quite intimidated when we first moved onto the North Cray because it was all very new and big and a lot of the travelling community lived in the area. It felt like my first day at school all over again because it seemed as though all the children my age knew each other. I worried again about fitting in, but about a week after we arrived I was down at the local park and I joined in a football game. Before I knew it I was hanging around with the local gang of kids all the time. Every night after school I'd go down to the park and mess around and play. I went from being a nobody at school to being a part of something cool. Everyone on the estate was hard and fighting was the main method of communication; I knew they all had my back.

The main ringleader was a girl called Tammy and I really looked up to her. She was younger than me but she was clearly in charge of everyone. We used to play Knock Down Ginger and Garden Hop, where we would race each other through our neighbours' gardens and try and not get caught. People would be sat in their front rooms watching telly and they'd see someone zoom past their window like a rocket. Another thing we'd do a lot was make funny phone calls. We'd go to the phone box and call a random number and say, 'Is Mr Wall there please?' and they'd said no. And we'd say, 'Is Mrs Wall there please?' and they'd say no. So then we'd say, 'Are any of the Walls there?' and when they said, 'No', we'd all shout together, 'Well how does your house stand up then?' I think that was quite a common gag around that time.

We lived right near a park called The Five Arches, which had shallow rivers and big trees and we hung out there a lot. I would 'go out' with a lad one minute, then we'd break up and I'd be going out with another boy by the end of the day. We didn't ever kiss each other but we'd call each other 'boyfriend' and 'girlfriend'. My first *proper* kiss was when I was 11, with a guy called James Carter who had a skinhead. It happened in someone's shed and I don't think we were a match made in heaven, but I was so proud I'd finally had a full-on snog.

I desperately wanted a bike back then because all the local kids had one. They used to come and call for me on their BMXs and I could never go out riding with them. I begged my parents to get me one and in the end they relented – and bought me a fold-up bike. Of all the bikes they could have got me! It looked like a commuter bike and I was so embarrassed I refused to ride it. I know my parents meant well because they thought it would be good for me to take it when we went to visit my grandparents, but it was no BMX.

Thankfully, shortly after we moved to North Cray I *finally* stopped wetting myself and it was such a relief to feel 'normal' for the first time in my life. None of the experts I went to see could ever explain what caused it, and I have no idea what made it stop. It just kind of fizzled out, and I was so bloody happy when it did.

I missed our old house but I liked my new friends and my new bedroom, so that kind of made up for it. For some reason back then I really wanted to be American, so my room was covered in American flags and anything else America-related I could get my hands on. I even spoke in an American accent sometimes. I had a few posters up as well, mainly of East 17, who I was obsessed with. Brian Harvey was my favourite but I actually ended up snogging another band member, Terry, much later on down the line when my friend Zoe and I went to London to pretty much stalk the band. I loved East 17 so much I even wanted to hold a peace concert in my back garden between them and Take That because I was sick of them arguing all the time. I just wanted them to be happy.

Funnily enough I also met Take That when I was younger. I went along to a concert in Crystal Palace where they were playing before they made it big. It was one of their first ever gigs and my mum said I couldn't go, but I sneaked out and went anyway. It was so hot that day they were throwing water over the crowd to try and keep us cool. I was right at the front of the stage and I got squashed and I couldn't breathe, so I got pulled over the barrier into the pit right in front while Take That were performing. It was when Robbie used to have a dummy round his neck all the time, and he gave me the one he was wearing that day because the band felt so bad about me getting crushed. I saw Robbie again at Soccer Aid in June 2014 and I talked to him about it. He remembers that day really well, but not surprisingly he didn't remember me!

So my bedroom was basically a mix of American memorabilia and boy bands. My brothers shared a bedroom and they had a futon sofa each, and my parents had another bedroom. The fourth bedroom was where my dad kept all of his instruments and I always used to come home from school and go straight in there to play on them (while being *very* careful not to damage anything).

My dad used to drink Colt 45 Malt Liquor and we had these massive Colt 45 cushions on our sofa. If you drank enough cans you could send off tokens and get different gifts from a catalogue and they were his pride and joy. My dad used to drink a lot, and if my mum was in the mood she did too. I don't remember a lot about that in my very early years, but there were always musicians around the house and drink was always a part of that. There was rarely a non-alcoholic moment in our house.

My dad's drinking got worse when we moved to North Cray, and when my parents rowed as a result I was often left in the middle of it all. My brothers were old enough to go out on their own, so they'd be hanging around the estate getting into all sorts of trouble and I'd be stuck in the house with the arguments. I used to sit on the stairs and watch them through the bannisters. I had to witness my mum and dad arguing and getting physically violent with each other so many times and I couldn't do anything about it.

My mum is left-handed and if my dad was drunk enough he'd forget and try to block her right arm and end up with a black eye. My dad never hit my mum and he never hit any of us, but my mum didn't have much control when she drank so she'd lash out. I remember going into the living room and literally banging their heads together once. I was only about 12 but it was the only thing I could think of doing to try and make them stop. I used to cry and beg them not to throw things at each other, but when they were in full flow there was nothing anyone could do.

In the end the only thing I discovered would make them take notice of me was if I took their bottles of booze into the kitchen and threatened to pour them away. As soon as I did that they would behave because they were so scared I was going to waste their alcohol. The hatred that came out when they had drink in their systems was unbelievable, but the next day it would all be forgotten and we'd be back to normal again. You weren't allowed to mention anything about it and it was as if it had never happened. I knew not to say anything because Mum and Dad would get really angry. Everything was brushed under the carpet until next time. They would be totally fine with each other and smile and say, 'Have a lovely day. See you later!' I found it so confusing.

It was the same with my brothers. They got away with murder because my parents gave up trying to keep them on the straight and narrow. If ever I was off school ill, I knew that the minute my mum went to work my brothers would magically reappear having bunked off. About half an hour later their girlfriends would turn up and they'd sit around watching TV and snogging. One time they tied me to a tree in the garden because I was being an annoying younger sister and asking their girlfriends all kinds of questions. They left me out there for hours; every now and again they'd pop out and give me some food and then disappear back inside. I must have driven them up the wall. I was always sneaking into their rooms to play their computer games and borrowing their stuff.

Even when I reached my early teens I liked being laddish and I used to go fishing with my friends. I kept a pot of maggots underneath my bed and one day when my mum was cleaning she heard a noise coming from it. She opened the box and hundreds of flies flew out and I don't think she's ever forgiven me. I wasn't allowed to fish again after that and as I was such a tomboy I was gutted. My mum was always trying to make me more girlie but I wasn't having any of it. One of my favourite items of clothing was a tracksuit that said 'Here comes trouble' on it. And I loved trainers. I'm not even sure I owned any dresses back then.

Things were so up and down with my parents and I'll never forget sitting in our living room one day when the phone rang. My mum picked it up, listened to whatever the person had to say, put the phone down and then went for my dad. I've never seen her look so furious. The caller was a woman called Jenny who claimed she'd had an affair with my dad ten years previously. My dad owned up to it and my parents had a blazing row. After that my dad disappeared for about five weeks. To this day I still don't know if my mum chucked him out or if he went to detox. I just know that he wasn't around for a while. Sometimes he'd disappear for a while and Mum used to tell us he was working away from home and I have no idea if he really was or not. Even though they had this ridiculously volatile relationship she was happier once he was back home. It was a classic case of 'can't live with each other, can't live without'.

My parents always had a massive stock of alcohol in their drinks cabinet at all times. Sometimes I'd take the vodka bottles into the kitchen, pour half of it away and fill the rest up with water and they had no idea. They both used to have Five Alive as a mixer and it had a pretty strong flavour, so thankfully they didn't notice. Dad also had crates of Special Brew and when I got to about 13 I'd be able to sneak the odd can out of the house because my dad was too drunk to notice. I'd go over to the park and share it with my mates, but it tasted like lighter fuel and I'd be plastered after a few sips.

I used to try and roll my dad's fags for him sometimes when he passed out, and the first time I ever did it they looked like big fat cigars. When he woke up he smoked one, probably out of politeness, and nearly singed his eyebrows. Both my parents smoked and from the age of about 11 Mum used to send me up to the corner shop with a note saying 'Can

Sam please have 20 Superkings. Thank you, Mrs Bailey.' You couldn't get away with doing that these days!

I begged my dad to stop drinking so many times. I'd come home from school and random people would be sitting in our house drinking and smoking wacky baccy at 3.30 in the afternoon. I think that was the norm for a lot of musician types and I guess I didn't know any difference. Dad wasn't a pub drinker; he liked being at home, which meant that after he'd had a few drinks his mates would turn up with their bongos and guitars and they'd all have a jamming session and get wasted. Sometimes I'd stay up with them because it was so noisy I knew that if I went to bed I wouldn't be able to sleep anyway.

As a result of what I witnessed when I was growing up, I barely touch alcohol now. The last time I got drunk was in 2008 and that was because I was drinking cocktails and they didn't taste like they had any booze in them. If my husband and I go out I may have one WKD vodka, but he knows that after a few sips I'll pass it to him. He can always tell when I've had enough and he'll look at me and say, 'Ready?' and I'll hand it over. I don't even like being around booze now, and my husband knows I don't like him drinking in front of the children or getting drunk if I'm in the house. He can do what he likes when he goes out, but we don't have alcohol in the fridge unless we're having people over. I've always said to him that if he comes home and goes straight to the fridge for a beer we're over, because I know how it starts. I've seen it first-hand.

CHAPTER 2

BORN TO RUN

With all of the drinking and fighting that was going on at home, it was important for me to have an outlet and a reason to get away from everything, and that was, and remained, sport. When I was 13 I started going to a local youth club. It was 25p to get in and they had a boys' football team I really wanted to play for. I had long wavy hair all the way down my back like Julia Roberts in *Pretty Woman*, but the boys said the only way I could play for them was if I cut it all off. I was so desperate to be on the team I went home, got a pair of scissors and chopped off the lot. My mum went ballistic and took me to the hairdressers where they cut my hair into a short style. I had curtains, a long fringe, which were really in with lads at the time, so I basically looked like a small boy. But it did mean I got to play for that team for two seasons as a forward, so it was well worth it. It was only when I started developing boobs that I had to call it a day because I couldn't get away with looking like one of the guys any longer.

Thankfully, soon after I left the lads' team they started a girls' team, so it all worked out perfectly and I was able to grow my hair again, much to my mum's delight. The local kids and I also used to play football in the park a lot. We graffitied a goal onto a wall and even though the area was full of bits of broken glass and empty crisp packets it was our place, and we loved it. I'd come home from school, watch *Grange Hill*, have my tea and go down straight to the park until it got dark. My mum even sent a letter to my school saying that I didn't want to play netball; I wanted to play football, which opened up a can of worms. Loads of other girls decided they wanted to do the same and it was a proper headache for the PE teachers.

Even though it wasn't easy at times, I had some brilliant moments living in North Cray. Every Friday my dad would bring home a McDonald's or KFC and we'd have dinner as a family. We also used to have what we called 'Henry VIII dinners'. Mum would make a leg of lamb, potatoes and vegetables and we'd sit on the floor in the living room and eat the lot. You weren't allowed to use a knife and fork and we drank out of silver goblets. We'd play folk music in the background, and then after dinner we'd watch a film Mum had hired from the video shop. Growing up, that was one of my absolute favourite things to do.

On Christmas day we would all sit round the table for lunch – if my mum hadn't passed out by then – and put all our names in a hat. You had to act like the person whose name you'd pulled out for the entire meal. Whoever pulled my name out would fidget and talk a lot of rubbish and go to the toilet a lot. If you were pretending to be one of my brothers you'd act like you were on *Kevin & Perry Go Large*. Us kids always wanted to be my dad so we could get away with swearing. I loved being able to shout, 'Pass the fucking gravy!' Whoever was my mum would obviously pretend to be completely drunk, and it was the one day where we got to see how we truly all saw each other.

Christmas was always brilliant fun, despite the drinking. We'd all get a black bin liner full of presents at the end of our beds every year (even when we were far too old for them!) and I used to get so excited the night before knowing what I was going to wake up to. One year I asked for these really cool LA Gear high-top trainers and I was the happiest girl alive when I got them. On Boxing Day we went to visit some friends of my parents' in Crystal Palace and my cousin David and I went to the park. I got really muddy, so I left my trainers outside the front door and someone nicked them! I was so upset.

The next year I asked my nan for some Nike trainers, but when I unwrapped them they were these awful plastic 'Nicks' she'd probably got from the market. They looked like clowns' trainers and my brothers found it hilarious. I didn't want to hurt my nan's feelings so I had to wear them all day and I looked ridiculous clomping round the house in these giant, brightly coloured shoes.

One year when I was in my teens my mum thought it would be really funny to get my nan a vibrator. It was only a small silver one and my parents told her it was a drinks stirrer. She had no idea and when we all went round for drinks on Boxing Day she was using it to stir everyone's drinks and we were in hysterics. We never did tell her what it was *really* for.

I think my parents only regret at moving to North Cray was that my brothers got in with a really bad crowd and became involved with drugs and all sorts. Charlie could handle himself but even though Danny was much bigger he wasn't as tough, so Charlie always took the lead. They felt a need to fit in because they knew they'd be targets for the local gangs if they weren't a part of it. Peer pressure was a big part in their downfall because they did things they probably would never have done if we'd stayed in our old house. They were doing a lot of acid and getting into fights; my mum used to despair but there was nothing she could do. By this time the boys were in their mid-teens and as anyone who's got teenagers knows, there's no telling them.

I started to get into a bit of trouble myself when high school rolled around. The first one I went to was called St Mary's and St Joseph's, which my mum chose because a lot of the kids from my primary school were going there.

Kate Bush also went there when she was young, which I always found quite exciting. I formed my first band there. We didn't have a name or anything; we just used to meet up and have jamming sessions in the music room. I played the drums, a lad called Martin Molly played piano, and another guy called Steven Austin was a violinist but he was learning guitar. Steven was my boyfriend for a short time but then he split up with me to go out with another girl called Siobhan for a week, the cad. Then he decided he wanted to get back with me for a week, and then he went back to Siobhan, and the pattern continued for several weeks. At one point he made us have a physical fight over him to decide who would win his heart. I won but he definitely wasn't worth it!

The first few months of high school were hard because, again, I got bullied. Also, Jenny, the woman my dad had the affair with, had two children at my school, which felt a bit weird. One day I was walking home and Jenny kerb-crawled me and started shouting abuse out of her car window, calling my mum all sorts of names. When I told mum she went mad and said I couldn't stay at the school, which I felt relieved about if I'm being honest. I didn't have any real friends there and I felt different somehow. I was still into sports and I did a lot of athletics and played hockey for the school. I had county trials and all sorts, but I still didn't feel good enough.

I even started doing a little bit of singing so I could try and get in with the cool group because the leader of the gang,

Rebecca, loved singing and she was the one who bullied me the most. But rather than make her warm to me it made her like me even less because she felt she had to compete against me. I didn't think I had a very good voice back then, but she obviously saw me as a threat and was constantly trying to outdo me. Once after PE we were in the changing rooms and she punched me square in the face for no reason at all and gave me a nosebleed. It made me feel so crap about myself, and rather than rush to my aid the other girls ignored me in case she turned on them too.

All I wanted to do was grow up, get a pair of boobs and start my periods so I could be like the other girls. They would all be in the changing rooms after sports showing off their bras and talking about their periods, and my own didn't start until quite late in life, so I felt like the odd one out. I remember wanting to be grown up so much I nicked one of my mum's Tampax to try it out and I was found collapsed on the bathroom floor. I was taken to hospital and it turned out I had toxic shock syndrome and I was told I could never use them again. That was the last time I did anything like that!

Thankfully, within 48 hours of the Jenny incident I had been moved to a new school, Cleeve Park, where a lot of my friends from the estate went. I walked in there on my first day and I said to myself, 'You need to make a difference today. You've got to make it clear to people that you are *not* going to be bullied.' The minute one girl came up and gave me a bit of attitude for being the new girl, that was it. I followed her down the corridor and pushed her really hard so she fell over. Everyone was standing around shouting 'fight, fight' and cheering. We totally laid into each other and were both punching each other repeatedly. It was my first proper fight and I was scared, but equally I had to let people know that I could stand up for myself.

I was sent home that day with a stern note and my parents weren't happy, but I think they kind of knew why I'd done it. I was sat watching telly in the living room with a giant lump on my head when dad turned to me and said, 'So, you had a fight today then. I see you head-butted her?' I was waiting for him to send me to my room and tell me girls shouldn't fight, but instead he sighed, 'You're doing it all wrong, come here', and he stood up and taught me the proper way to head-butt someone, telling me, 'Short, sharp shock.' I think he realised that I needed to be able to handle myself. He didn't want me to be the kid who was forever getting beaten up.

You had to have your wits about you at Cleeve Park. A lot of the travelling community went there and I had to toughen up quickly, but after that day no one bullied me. In fact on a few occasions I became the bully to prove my worth to other people, which I'm really ashamed of now. If I could go back and change it I would. I'll never forget this one kid who was sitting down and for some reason everyone was spitting on him. I walked up and I spat on him too, to show that I was as hard as everyone. That poor kid was probably so traumatised. I know how I'd been affected by the horrible things that happened to me and I really wish I'd stuck up for him instead of joining in.

I was never the ringleader and despite that fight on the first day I never actually *started* any fights because it wasn't in my nature to behave like that. I'd be one of the ones in the background going, 'Yeah! Whatever she said!' But if things kicked off we'd all pile in. I remember a big fight breaking out and someone lending me some sovereign rings because travellers used to wear a lot of gold. I punched this girl and when I looked down at one of the rings I couldn't see the coin because it was covered in blood. It was horrific. I've still got scars on my hands from where I wore those rings when I was fighting. I guess I did what any normal 13- or 14-year-old in that situation would do. I kept my wits about me and I stayed on the safest side.

Aside from the fighting, Cleeve Park was a fantastic school. The teachers were amazing and Mr Pike, the maths teacher, was my absolute favourite. He had a yellow rubber duck and if someone wasn't paying attention he would throw it at them and shout 'Duck!' Teachers couldn't get away with doing that now but it was what kept us in check in the classroom. He talked to us like we were adults and not kids and because of that we had a lot more respect for him and most of the time actually did behave.

I carried on with my cross-country running at Cleeve Park and I ran in the Bexley and English Championships. I also went on to run for England in the European Championships. I was still a tiny little thing, so I was very fast. I was in Dartford Harriers Athletics Club for a while, but I didn't like it because they took everything far too seriously. I just wanted to have a laugh and run, not have loads of pressure heaped on me.

When I was 15 I went on my first ever holiday without my parents. I went to a Haven holiday park with some of my mates from the estate and I'd had to beg my mum to let me go. While I was there I fell head over heels (well, trainers in my case) for one of the Haven Mates. Nothing happened between us but on the last night we slow danced to 'Superwoman' by Karyn White together and I was on cloud nine. I kept singing it for days afterwards, and from then on every day when I was with my mates they'd ask me sing it for them. That's when I first really started to get the singing bug. My friends kept telling me how good I was and finally I started to believe that they could be right.

After that I started singing at home in my bedroom, and also writing songs. I didn't have any professional lessons but I started teaching myself to sing like the big divas. I'd write down the lyrics to songs and I'd use a red star to mark wherever Mariah or Whitney breathed, and then I'd try and do the same as them with a backing track. The first song I wrote was called 'I'm So In Love With You', and it's the most hideous thing you've ever heard. I will never, ever sing it again as long as I live. But back then I thought I was the next

Mariah Carey, so I proudly sang it for my parents. Afterwards my mum said I should start entering talent competitions. It wasn't something I'd ever thought about until then, but I had nothing to lose. I still wasn't very confident in myself but for some reason when I sang it made me feel better. I wanted people other than my mum and friends to tell me that singing was the path I should be taking. Mum always used to say, 'Oh, you sound just like that Mariah McCrarey.' She could never say her name right and I still don't think she can. She always gushed about how wonderful I was, but all I'd get from my dad was a measured nod and sometimes he'd say, 'That was fucking handsome.' He wasn't the type to go over the top.

The first competition I entered was Bexley's 'Search For A Star' competition at Crayford Town Hall. I sang 'I'm So In Love With You' and, knowing me back then, either Whitney Houston's 'Greatest Love of All' or Mariah Carey's 'Hero'. I also played the drums and I had to put my dad's coat over my legs because, amazingly, I was wearing a dress and I didn't want to flash everyone. If I remember rightly it was one of Mum's dresses because she said I should look a bit glam!

I ended up coming first and I'm sure there are some very dodgy pictures of me from that day out there somewhere. My parents were so proud of me. I think I was their last hope. My brothers were still wayward and flitting between jobs. Danny wanted to be a chef and Charlie wanted to be a footballer, so they did have aspirations when they were young, but they were forever getting into trouble. If they weren't fighting with each other they'd be fighting with someone else and they didn't have the best reputation.

I was so buoyed up by my win I started entering more and more competitions. I went in for one in Deptford and one of the members of Damage was on the judging panel, which to my mind meant it was akin to being on TV. I won there too and when people said to me I should sing professionally it made me feel amazing. I sang anywhere and everywhere I could.

My parents would send me up the chippy on a Friday night and there would be karaoke on in our local pub, The Albany. While I was waiting for the food to be ready I'd go in and sing a song. Then I'd disappear again and everyone would be left thinking 'Who the hell was that?' I'd get a round of applause and then go and get my chips. I started entering local karaoke competitions when I was out with my friends without my parents knowing. I used to come home with a trophy and a £50 note having just won. I used to get £5 pocket money every Saturday, so that £50 was a hell of a lot of money to me.

When I was young I used to spend all of my pocket money on sweets, but as I got older my friends and I started pooling our money and going to the off-licence. We'd wait for someone older to come along and ask them to buy us alcohol, but I rarely used to drink mine. I'd pour it away when no one was looking and pretend to be pissed because

I didn't like the taste or what it did to people. One of the rare times I did get drunk was when I was going out with a lad called Grahame Pink who had a motorbike. He gave me a lift home one night and I was leaning to the side trying to get some air because I was so plastered. I went straight upstairs and lay on my bed face down and I felt awful the next day. My hand/eye coordination used to go after a few drinks and I remember sticking a burger in my eye instead of my mouth once because I was seeing double. Me and booze definitely do not mix.

Drinking didn't ever feel like fun for me, even when we started to go to under-18s clubs. I started wearing all of the luminous clothing that was really fashionable at the time. I'd built up a collection of luminous sunglasses which were given away free with McDonald's Happy Meals, so I always had a pair of those on. I also had ra-ra skirt, which I wore very occasionally, and loads of shell suits. There was also a really cool (for the time) silky tracksuit called Black and White. It came in loads of different colours and all my friends and I had one. We looked like a bloody girl band with our Fila and LA Gear trainers or Wallabies. My mum and dad didn't have a pot to piss in, but my mum would spend every last penny she had making sure I had something nice to wear so I could fit in with the other kids.

My brothers were really into acid house, so they were always out clubbing wearing stupid clothes. My parents had allowed them to have a mural on a wall in their bedroom, so they'd painted a ridiculous Union Jack with a British Bulldog in the middle of it. I came home one day and heard all of these noises coming from their room. I pushed open the door and before I knew what was happening one of them had grabbed me and thrown me onto the futon. When I looked up they were both standing there shaking. They were tripping on acid and they thought the British Bulldog was coming out of the wall and trying to lick them. They were trying to explain to me what was happening to them, but I'd never tried drugs at that point so I couldn't really get my head around it. In the end I had to literally pull them out of the room one by one. It was like something out of *Poltergeist*. They were absolutely terrified. Not surprisingly, that put me off trying acid for life.

I did, however, start smoking when I was 15. Either a group of us used to buy ten Benson and Hedges between us (which cost £1.10!) or I'd nick my mum's fags and go down the alley with my friend Maria. We'd smoke as quickly as we could so we didn't get caught. If there was a group of us smoking in the playground we'd play chew the butt, where everyone had to take a drag of a fag and then pass it to the next person. Whoever was holding the cigarette when it finally went out had to chew the butt. I have no idea why we did it but everyone did back then.

When I was 15 we moved again, to Albany Park in Bexley, which was a safer place to live in that there were fewer fights and break-ins. It was near enough our old place that I could still hang out with my mates, so I wasn't too upset. By that time my brothers were moving in and out of home all the time. They wanted their own space and some freedom, so they rented bedsits together and I'd go round and visit them. They weren't always nice places but they were theirs and that's what mattered to them.

The first day we moved to Albany Park, Dad promised me that he would make sure he did my room up first and make it exactly how I wanted. I got some shabby chic furniture and he was going to put my bed up and make it look really cool. But then one of his mates came round with a few cans, and the next thing you knew he was drunk and my room was still filled with boxes. My mum was running around trying to unpack and get things done and I was so furious with my dad because he was doing bugger all. I was standing at the top of our bannister looking into our new living room and I could see him laughing and joking with his mate and I shouted, 'I hate you!' at him. He completely ignored me so I shouted it again. Once again he totally ignored me. I was at boiling point and I really wanted to get his attention, so I called him the 'C' word. It's the only time I've ever used that word and meant it because I loathe it, but it certainly got his attention. I ran into my room and slammed the door, and he came flying in a few seconds later.

I was so wound up I got him in a headlock and I was screaming all sorts of things at him. It had got to the point where I didn't feel like I was his priority anymore. Alcohol was. When I told him how I felt he was crushed. He was genuinely upset and I felt so bad, but thankfully it made him take a long hard look at himself and prompted him to go to rehab and get help. We all knew he was a full-blown alcoholic and it was heartbreaking to see how much he'd changed over the course of my life. He was like a shadow of the man he'd once been. His vibrancy had gone, he barely worked and he was constantly lethargic. He had to try and sort himself out.

My dad was in rehab for six weeks and to start with he did really well. But then one of his drinking 'mates' started visiting him and sneaking in beers. What a great friend, eh? Needless to say the treatment didn't work and he was soon back home, drinking beer after beer on the sofa. The big problem was that my dad was a nicer person when he was drunk. When he was sober he'd get the shakes and feel so ill he'd get really grumpy. As soon as he had a drink, he'd feel calm again and was much easier to be around. So he pretty much drank constantly when he was in the house.

One day, after a big session the previous night, my dad drove to the shop around the corner from us to get some cigarettes and he got stopped by the police. Even though he hadn't yet had a drink that day, he was still over the limit so he lost his driving licence. As a result of not being able to drive he was unable to work at all, which was the last thing he needed. Now he had an excuse to sit at home and drink full-time.

My mum was working as a market researcher by then. She had to stop people in the street and ask them about everything from cheese to cars. Now my dad didn't have a job she was grafting harder than ever and so she was knackered most of the time. One day she came home from work and I was playing one of my dad's acoustic guitars. She said she wasn't feeling well and the next thing I knew she was unconscious and her eyes were rolling into the back of her head. I screamed upstairs for my dad to come down and by the time he got downstairs mum's tongue had gone down the back of her throat and she was having a convulsion. We rang an ambulance and she was taken to hospital where they told us she'd had a fit because she was so run down. She had to take time off from work and I was so worried about her. I think she was physically and emotionally exhausted from working non-stop and worrying about my dad.

It didn't help that my parents were rowing more than ever. Dad still had his mates round all the time, making noise and drinking, and it was the last thing mum needed after being out all day working. I'd got to an age where my mum could be open with me about things and she started to say to me, 'I want to leave your dad.' I felt like I was being disloyal to dad but I'd say to her, 'Well, do it then. You've got to do what's right for you.' I knew they would be better off apart because dad was becoming more and more difficult. Mum would take ages cooking him a dinner and he'd take it and throw it on the floor to wind her up. They really knew how to push each other's buttons. But for some reason she couldn't walk away. Not until much later on anyway.

Looking back on my childhood now, I wouldn't change a thing. Not even the bullying. Now I've got kids myself I can empathise if they're having a hard time at school because I've been through it myself. I would know the signs if they were being bullied and I would be able to talk to them about it. I've spoken to my children about bullying and how much it affected me and they know it's not a nice thing to do. My daughter Brooke is in the same class as a girl who has learning difficulties and she helps her whenever she can. She understands that if she's got the means to help someone, she should. I really hope those values stay with her throughout her life.

Every single thing that happened to me when I was a young kid and a teenager has made me who I am now. Because I had to cope with my parents non-stop arguing growing up, I make sure Craig and I talk to each other about everything now. I don't ever want to end up in the same position my parents were in because they stopped communicating with each other. It was horrible to see them fall apart, so anytime Craig and I have a problem, we talk it through.

People still say to me now, 'You had it tough as a kid', but I didn't know any different. If I'd lived in a namby-pamby house and skipped over to the park every day I wouldn't be anywhere near as strong as I am now. I can stick up for myself and it's also kept me grounded. I treat other people as I want to be treated, so I'm always nice and I'm always respectful. I really do believe you get back what you give out in life and there's never a reason to be rude to anyone.

CHAPTER 3

SCHOOL'S OUT

I was nearing the end of my school days and my GCSEs were coming up. My favourite subjects were music, English and cookery. I hated IT and French, mainly because our French teacher used to pick his nose and wipe it on his desk and it made me feel sick. Annoyingly, they didn't bring drama and PE GCSEs in until the year after I finished, so they weren't available. I didn't do very well in my exams and the best grade I got was a C in music. I can't read music but I can play it by ear.

I didn't really care too much about my grades because my plan was either to become a footballer or go to drama school. In the end I decided to apply to Bexley College to do a BTEC diploma in performing arts. I can't remember much about the audition but I know I had to do a little bit of acting and singing, and I was so happy when I was offered a place.

I was expecting there to be a massive class full of people, but when I walked in there were only eight of us. It was a really eclectic mixture of people. I got on really well with one girl, Michelle, from the word go. She had her own bedsit in Thamesmead, so there were no parents around when I went there and we could pretty much do what we wanted, which is a very exciting prospect at 16. She looked after horses; I'd help her muck out before college and we became really, really good friends. I spent so much time at her place I was hardly at home, which was definitely a good thing with my parents the way they were.

We started going out clubbing in London with other friends to places like Club UK and Bagleys. I was in Club UK one night when I saw a guy walking around marking people on their backs with some kind of pen. I couldn't really see what he was doing because it was dark, and the people he was marking were far too gone to notice what was happening. About 15 minutes later the music stopped and the police came in. They took away the people who had marks on their backs, and then the club carried on. It must have been the quickest raid known to man.

Another time I was there, this poor girl was so off her nut a group of lads started stripping off her clothes on the dance floor. It was clear she was too wasted to stop them and everyone else was either ignoring the situation or laughing. Because I was sober I stormed in, grabbed her and took her off to the toilet to get her dressed. Then I got one of the bouncers to take care of her and call her a taxi home because anything could have happened to her. I really can't imagine what appeals to people about feeling that out of control.

Even now I'm always the one who gets my friends home safely after a night out. I can go out with £30 in my purse and come back with £28 because all I need is a soft drink. I'll be the one who can remember everything the next day and I always take the mickey out of my mates for all of the stupid things they've done. We'll have a right laugh about it and I'll be safe in the knowledge that I didn't do anything ridiculous. I love that feeling. People are always trying to get me drunk because they think I'll be funny, but I don't think my mum or Craig have seen me pissed once. Tipsy maybe, but never hammered. I don't change much after a drink; I just get friendlier. I'll sit on people's laps and cuddle everyone, so it would probably be a bit dangerous if I *was* a full-on pisshead!

Like drinking, drugs were never something I was that bothered about. I'll hold my hands up and admit that I did try certain drugs in my younger years. I remember trying puff for the first time when my brothers were living in one of their bedsits. I went round to visit them and one of their mates thought it would be funny to give me a spliff. Obviously I tried to act like I was all grown up and had done it loads of times before, so I took several puffs and then laughed a lot and fell asleep. That was the last time I bothered with that. What's the point in smoking something that's going to make you pass out? Another time I 'tried' something was when I got spiked when I was 16. I was in our local pub and there were a group of lads on the next table who were all laughing at me. I couldn't understand why so I ignored them. I went outside to play football in the beer garden and when someone kicked the ball to me it stopped in front of me and said, 'Kick me!' in a really loud, deep voice.

I freaked out and went and sat underneath a tree to try and calm down, but I thought the tree was alive and was trying to grab me. Everything I saw was evil and everyday objects were turning into monsters with sharp teeth and evil eyes. Luckily some of my friends realised I'd been spiked and they took me to the hospital. I was put on a drip and I had to stay in for a few hours until I was back to 'normal'. It was one of the worst experiences of my life. It turned out one of those boys had been boasting about spiking me but no one person would take the blame, so my brothers ended up punching every single one of them just to make sure they got the right person. But despite that incident, like most teenagers, I still experimented. When we went out I would be the only person who didn't drink and everyone else would be having a good time but by 1am I'd be shattered and sober. We wouldn't finish until seven or eight in the morning and I didn't drive so I couldn't get myself home, which meant I'd have to wait for my mates so we could all get one of the first trains home together.

One day one of my friends said to me 'Why don't you take something to keep you awake and give you more energy?' What she offered me was speed. I'd never tried it before but it did do exactly what she said. The side effects were awful. I was thin anyway and the drugs made me not to want to eat, and I wouldn't be able to sleep so I felt like rubbish the next day. The next time I went out clubbing again I'd end up doing the same thing. I got into a really negative pattern for a short while.

A lot of people I knew were doing ecstasy, which frightened the living daylights out of me. Because of peer pressure I tried it and I didn't like it at all. I only really tried drugs because everyone else around me was doing them. Back then I was more of a follower than a leader. I guess I didn't want to be the only one not doing anything and felt a certain amount of pressure to fit in.

Everything was so readily available. I was so lucky that I didn't like them because I know people who have got themselves into a lot of trouble where drugs were concerned.

I guess because I'd grown up around all the alcohol and with my brothers doing drugs and seen the damage it did it put me off going down the same path. I was always aware that things could potentially tip over and I could end up liking things that weren't good for me just a little bit *too* much.

Thankfully the only things I've ever been addicted to are chocolate and cigarettes and I feel so grateful that I don't have that self-destructive gene. My family almost showed me what *not* to do.

People drink or do drugs so they can escape, but I didn't have any need to. I was always very outgoing and I was happy with myself, so what was the point in doing things that made me feel bad about myself and guilty? It made no sense. Another red flag for me was when a guy I'd known at school took something without finding out what it was. Tragically it gave him brain damage and he now has the mental age of a 13-year-old.

I certainly wasn't an angel when I was younger and I didn't walk around with a halo on my head, and I did what I did because of the people who I hung out with. It scares me that these days apparently you can buy an ecstasy tablet for about £3. It's cheaper than buying a glass of wine. It's shocking.

I'm glad there is so much more information available now and a lot of anti-drug campaigns which really hit home to people. All those years ago people were taking drugs and they didn't really know the dangers, but now everything is very transparent and you know that if you do drugs you're taking a huge risk.

Some people will assume that once you're famous it's all sex, drugs and rock and roll but I can honestly say that I haven't been offered drugs since I've been in the public eye. I think it's quite clear I'm not that kind of person so that's probably why. I would much rather have a cup of tea and an early night and I think people are well aware of that.

Bexley College was a bit of a strange time. I think because I was going out so much and staying with Michelle all the time, it feels like a bit of a blur. It wasn't all jazz hands (people walking around being over the top and showbiz) and am-dram like I'd expected; it was pretty laid back. We did a few shows and around Christmas time we put on a production called *Cindy Ryella*, an Essex-girl version of *Cinderella*. Michelle and I played the ugly sisters Sharon and Tracy, and I remember us getting on a bus in our outfits, which consisted of a pink mini-skirt, fur coat and tons of make-up. We stayed in character all the way and everyone on the bus was giggling at us.

I knew everyone's lines in the play because I recorded the whole thing on my little karaoke machine at home using different voices for different characters. Then I left blank the parts where my lines were supposed to be. I used to play it back over and over again and speak my lines during the blank bits. I took that tape with me everywhere and by the time we performed the show to an audience I knew the entire thing inside out. At the time we thought the show was West End quality, but if I were to watch it back now I bet it would be bloody awful.

That karaoke machine was a godsend because I also learnt to harmonise using it. I used to record an entire verse of a song, like Take That's 'Pray', and then play it back. Then I'd put another tape in the other side of the machine and sing over the top of it, so I was harmonising with myself. I used to do it over and over again and I had all of these tapes filled with different songs.

I managed to get my diploma at the end of my year-long course, but the whole thing was so relaxed it was more of a laugh than anything. It was the first time I'd been treated like an adult and there was no one taking a register, so I could get away with being late and messing around because no one told you off. If we'd been out clubbing the night before, Michelle and I would roll up around lunchtime and the tutors didn't say a word. We kind of made our own rules and I loved that.

Because I'd passed the course I got the opportunity to try out for the Miskin Theatre, which was based in North West Kent College in Dartford. I got accepted and Michelle also got offered a place. We were still good mates but I'd started to kind of distance myself from her a bit. She was still partying a lot and I wanted to get my head down and work hard. I'd had my year of messing around and now I wanted to learn as much as I could about performing.

On my first day at Miskin Theatre we were told we had to decide if we wanted to do acting, dancing or music, and not surprisingly I chose music. I met a girl called Lucy on the course and we had so much in common. We started working together a lot and from then on we were pretty much inseparable. She used to hang out in a local pub called The White Swan, so I started spending a lot of time there too. I also got a job collecting glasses in The Albany, so, ironically, I ended up spending most of my time in pubs.

One day we were in The White Swan and a guy called Shaun Williamson was performing, whose name you may recognise. He lived opposite the pub in a tiny cottage with his girlfriend Mel and he was well-known locally. We became good friends and he very kindly invited me to sing in the pub whenever he did. He was also doing some other small paid gigs locally and asked if I wanted to perform with him at those. They became my first paid performing work. It made me feel much more confident about my singing. If people were willing to pay to hear me, I couldn't be that bad, could I?

Shaun is also an actor, and within a few months he was offered the role of Barry on *EastEnders*. It meant he had to give up the pub singing, so he offered to lend me his PA system so I could go out on my own. It was such a lovely offer but at 17 I felt I was too young to fly solo, so instead he gave me some blank Mariah Carey backing tracks to practice at home with. I have a lot to thank him for.

Shortly afterwards, my Uncle Paul offered to pay for me to go into a professional music studio and record some tracks. It was something I'd been desperate to do for ages. Those sessions led to me singing on a dance track for an old school friend of mine called Matt Zillwood. I loved that because I could be completely anonymous. I got to sing but no one knew it was me, which was ideal. I know it may sound hard to believe but it was never my plan to be famous. I originally wanted to be a backing vocalist and I still love the idea of it now. I would love to sing back-up for someone like Adele, and feel important because I'm a part of something but not have all of the attention on me. Obviously that's not how things have worked out, and I wouldn't change what's happened to me for the world, but certainly in the early years I was far too self-conscious and lacking in confidence to think I could ever be well known in my own right.

Not only did The White Swan provide me with my first paid singing work, it was also where I met my first serious boyfriend, Darren. There isn't any big romantic story behind it. I think he bought me a drink and we had a chat and that was it, we were a couple. He lived with his nan and granddad, who were lovely people, and I was round there constantly. I was absolutely smitten and it was much more fun than being at home. I remember Darren having to meet my dad for the first time. Everyone was winding him up because they knew my dad would give him a hard time. He was nervous so I told him to take my dad some beers, and when he turned up with some Special Brew they were instantly best mates. It didn't take a lot to win my dad over!

Darren's nan and granddad ran a company which sourced homes for foreign students to stay in. My mum decided it would be a good way to make some extra money, so she started taking in students regularly. We used to have two staying at once and they had to be taken to the coach each day in Eltham, and then picked up and fed each evening. They had to speak English the whole time they were around us to improve their language skills and I think Mum liked it because it meant that Dad had to behave himself when they were around. We had so many students our front room started to look like a European knick-knack shop because they always bought us gifts, and sometimes we had a real laugh with them.

My mum's so generous and such a good host she would end up spending more money on the students than actually earning it. She used to buy them so much nice food and really take care of them. Because my brothers still lived at home some of the time, my mum had to be very particular about which students she hosted. She was terrified that one day some young French girl would come knocking on the door with a baby in her arms.

We had one girl staying who was about 15 and she was absolutely stunning. Danny really liked her and he was desperate to impress her. He was playing drums in a band down at the youth club, so he invited her along hoping that she'd think he was some kind of rock star. He'd been boasting to everyone about how amazing she was but when she turned up she was wearing a short skirt and clearly wasn't a fan of shaving. She had these really thick dark hairs covering her legs and once he saw them their romance was over before it had even begun.

In the end it turned out it wasn't the students Mum needed to watch out for when it came to Danny – it was the local girls. He'd been seeing a girl – we'll call her Jane – for a few months when she fell pregnant and eventually they had a son called Jason.

College was going well but after about six months I felt frustrated because I wanted to really get my teeth into something. I wanted to perform full time, so I applied to be a Redcoat at Butlins. I was really panicking about the audition and so Dad said he would come along with me and hold my hand. We travelled on the train to Minehead, which was quite a trek, and I asked my dad not to drink beforehand but promised I'd get him some beers for the train journey home. I kept my promise and when we got back to Albany Park station I headed to Darren's and Dad went home. A couple of hours later I got a phone call saying that Dad was in hospital – he'd fallen down a pothole outside our house and broken his leg in two places because he was drunk. He was in full plaster and from that day on he started to go even more downhill both mentally and physically. He couldn't walk for several weeks, and when he eventually got the plaster off, his leg didn't heal properly. It was very thin and had no muscle strength left in it, so he was in constant pain and let himself go more than ever. He didn't wash and he grew a big beard so he didn't have to bother to shave.

Rather than fight it and try and get help from the doctor to help heal his leg, he pretty much gave in. My mum was buying him beers all the time and making his dinner and all he did was sit around watching TV and feeling sorry for himself. My parents were arguing more than ever and as a result I pretty much lived round at Darren's house so I could escape from it all.

Because Dad's leg was so bad he used to crawl up the stairs when he needed to go to the toilet. But sometimes he'd be so drunk he wouldn't get there in time and he'd wet himself. He once weed in a plant pot because he was so hammered he couldn't move from the sofa. It was like he'd totally given up. He got so down that everything became a bit too much for him. It was so hard for my mum. She was out working and then she'd have to come home and cook and clean and look after him and of all of his tag-alongs, who would sit in the front room boozing and being loud. It was like a piece of my dad had broken along with his leg. I barely even recognised him.

I tried to talk to him and get him to see sense many times. I'd shout at him to pull himself together and we'd end up having a barney because I was so frustrated that he wouldn't help himself. He'd always been the person I looked up to, who helped to provide for his family and was strong, and now my mum had to do everything on her own. I'd beg him to sort himself out, but all he used to say was, 'Ring me from Barbados!' That was his way of telling me to live a bit before I tried to tell him what to do. His attitude was 'When you know a bit more about life and you've been around the world, then you can lecture me'. It was hard to see him falling apart but I knew that if he wanted to get better, he was the only one who could help himself.

Mum started talking about leaving him again and I couldn't put up any kind of argument about why she should stay apart from the fact that I was worried about how he would cope without her. But then maybe if she did leave him, I thought, it might make him see sense and get himself together? Mum had become really resentful towards him and there was such a terrible atmosphere in the house. They hardly ever smiled any more and they had a constant stream of visitors, so that they didn't have to talk to each other.

Sadly I didn't get the job at Butlins, but through word of mouth I got a job working as a support artist at Lakeside Country Club in Frimley Green, Camberley. It's a big venue and every Saturday night a comedy act such as Joe Pasquale, Bradley Walsh or Cannon and Ball performed. It was always packed and I'd go on before the main performer and sing six or seven songs as a warm-up. One night Joe Pasquale was performing and he was massively famous at the time. I really wanted to meet him, so I knocked on his dressing room door. He opened it in just his pants and invited me in. Darren was walking up just behind me but Joe didn't see him so he pretty much shut the door in his face. Oh dear.

I was in there for about half an hour eating sandwiches and having a laugh and I was far too excited about meeting Joe to worry about Darren being annoyed. Or the fact Joe was sitting there in his boxer shorts! Darren, meanwhile, was *incredibly* pissed off. In the car on the way home he was in a right mood because he genuinely thought that something

Above: My mum and dad looking very smart in their younger years.

Left: My favourite picture in the world: me and my dad sitting on the bonnet of his old car.

Above: Me with my brother Danny looking studious and well behaved for once!

Below left: Me aged three playfully trying to help out around the house.

Below right: Me and my mum. She loved putting me in smart dresses.

Above: Me with my brothers Danny and Charlie. Not too sure about the outfits, guys!

Below: Another stylish look. Well, it was the 80s…

Me and my nan and grandad, Rita and John (*above*). They loved coming to watch me sing. Here I am performing at the Frog & Nightgown pub on Old Kent Road in London (*below*).

Above: This is me singing at a fundraising event for Cancer Research.

Below: My mum and I when I was a Bluecoat in 1998. I was known as 'Sammy' back then.

Above: All aboard the *Thompson Sapphire, c.* 1998. I'm third from the back with an excited smile on my face.

Below: Here I am getting 'Employee of the Month' on board the *Sapphire* ship. It was a really proud moment.

We had a great time performing on the *Sapphire* and wore some, erm, interesting outfits. I'm in the middle of the second row.

Here I am dressed up for a 'Pop Goes the 80s' show. It was all about the big hair back then. I got through a lot of hairspray.

had gone on between Joe and myself. I bumped into Joe on the *Dancing on Ice* tour recently and said to him, 'You nearly split me and my other half up. He thought we were having a snogging session in your dressing room and I was only 17!' To be honest, if he had split us up he would have been doing me a favour. But back then I had no idea what was around the corner.

I was still playing a lot of football at this time, and I played for loads of different clubs over the years. The longest stretch I had was playing for London Women's and I really enjoyed it there. It became harder and harder to fit it in around work and seeing Darren, but I stuck with it because it meant the world to me, even though getting to away games was a nightmare because I didn't drive.

I became so busy with the football and music side of things that I decided to give up college completely. I felt like I'd learnt a lot but I wanted more practical, hands-on experience. I was only performing in the evenings, which meant that I was able to get a day job and start earning some proper money. I got a job in a café and I also worked with my mum doing market research to support me while I did gigs, both paid and unpaid. A couple of months later I got a job through one of Darren's friends working for a cable company in Lewisham called Videotron, which has now become Virgin Media. I was on a YTS scheme and felt so important travelling to work on the train each day wearing smart clothes. I'd been there a while when a job came up for a direct debit clerk, so I went for it and to my amazement was offered the job. I genuinely had no idea what a direct debit was!

I don't know how I blagged my way through the first few weeks, but I managed to get my head around the role and it was all going brilliantly. Well, until I got the sack, that is. My colleagues and I could instant message each other through our computers – I guess it was like an early form of emailing – but I didn't realise that the bosses could monitor them. I got called into my manager's office one day and he showed me this record of all the messages I'd sent, which showed I'd been blatantly messing around when I should have had my head down getting the job done. I wasn't that gutted because the job wasn't what I wanted to do for the rest of my life, but the one thing I had really enjoyed was when the police used to come in to get copies of phone records with reference to various crimes. We didn't have the Internet then, so it was all stored on a microfiche machine, and I had to go through everything and print off whatever they needed. I loved doing that – and I guess it gave me a bit of a taste of my future career.

My plan was still to carry on singing and somehow break into it full-time, but in the meantime I went back to doing market research. I had to do things like go into a shop and buy and bra, then take it back and fill in forms to say how well my complaint had been dealt with. I was a mystery shopper, mystery eater, mystery traveller – you name it. I had to go to Wembley and interview people outside a Bob Dylan concert to see who drank Carling beer. It wasn't all bad. Somehow I managed to blag a ticket, so I got to see him live, which was amazing!

Because I was bubbly, people were always saying to me I should work in a holiday camp, but because I hadn't been accepted as a Redcoat I felt a bit disillusioned with it all. Then a friend pointed out to me that if you get knocked down you have to get back up, and they were so right. I decided I had nothing to lose by auditioning to be a Bluecoat at Pontins. I was working the following day, so on my break I went to a phone box and called Pontins in Pakefield and asked to speak to the entertainments manager, Sam. The next thing I knew I was doing Frank Spencer impressions and telling jokes down the phone. When I finished Sam said to me, 'Congratulations, you've got a job.' I was in total shock.

I was so happy, but of course there was Darren to consider. I thought he was a keeper and that we'd be together forever. I thought I was in love with him, but knowing now what love really is I would say it was more of an infatuation. Still, I was torn as to what to do. I didn't want to miss out on the job but I also didn't want to leave Darren behind. Thankfully he made up my mind for me...

One Saturday night Darren and his mates went out on a big booze-up. My friend Rachel was going out with one of his mates, Paul, and she was convinced he was cheating on her. She asked me if I'd drive up to the pub in Bromley where they were drinking to spy on them with her. When we got there we sneaked up this gravel path to the beer garden and we could see them having a beer and a laugh. Nothing untoward was going on, so we didn't think any more of it. I went back home and waited for Darren, but when he didn't arrive I went to Paul's to see if he was there. Paul claimed he'd gone to a lock-in at The Albany, and I was so angry he hadn't let me know that I went up there to find him. However, I didn't just find him. When I walked round to the side of the pub, Darren was up against the wall with some girl who looked old enough to be his mother. I laid into the pair of them and she went scuttling off shouting something about Darren claiming he was single. I told him he could forget about ever coming near me again, and I ran off down the road.

I went straight back to his house and left a note for his nan and granddad saying: 'Darren and I have split up. Ask him why. Love you with all the world, Sam.' The next day Darren's nan phoned me and told me that Darren wouldn't come out of his room. She ask me to go round and see him and the only reason I agreed was because I needed to get all of my stuff back. When he opened the door to his bedroom, I was so taken aback. He was in tears and he'd had built a shrine to me with photos and candles. It was like I'd died. Instead of feeling sorry for him, I felt even angrier. He was full of self-pity when I was the one who had been wronged.

Incredibly, after a few weeks Darren did convince me to

get back with him. I knew I could never forgive him and I felt so resentful that he'd hurt me, but part of me still thought I loved him. Despite that, I knew that I couldn't put my plans on hold so I accepted the job at Pontins. Darren said that he needed to make some big changes too, so he decided to go travelling in Australia for six months. I hoped having some time apart might help me to forgive him.

CHAPTER 4

PUT ON YOUR
RED SHOES

I started working at Pontins in late 1997 and it was a whole new world to me. It was the first time I'd properly lived away from home and I had my very own room. It was only tiny but it had a bathroom and a little desk and it really did feel like a mini home for the time I was there. Even now the smell of Herbal Essences shampoo and conditioner takes me right back there in an instant because I always used to use it in the shower. All of the memories it brings up are good ones because I had the time of my life.

The other bluecoats and I lived side by side in a long line of chalets next to each other and there was always something going on. There were a lot of people going in and out of those rooms, if you get my drift. Even though it would have been so easy for me to pull guys, I was completely faithful to Darren. The guests loved the Bluecoats and a lot of them were very flirty, so there was plenty of opportunity to cheat, but it's not in my nature.

All of the other Bluecoats were copping off with people left, right and centre and I'll never forget one of the guys saying to me, 'Never pull anyone on the first night because there's a new intake of people every Friday and someone better may be among them.' That kind of sums up what it was like. Some of the other staff members even had star charts. The blokes were much worse than the women and I was so wide-eyed and innocent about it all.

Six weeks after I arrived there I got an airmail letter from Darren that was basically a Dear John. It was one of those letters that looks like an envelope but was actually a piece of paper that folded out, and some of the other Bluecoats thought it was really glamorous that I'd got a letter from the other side of the world. Darren wittered on about how great Australia was and then basically said he'd met someone and didn't want to be with me anymore. I was so annoyed! We'd been together for two years by then and he dumped me by letter. He couldn't even be brave enough to phone me. And I'd wasted all of those months being faithful when I could have been having a whale of a time!

I was sad that we'd split up but I was still holding on to some anger over his cheating, so there was definitely a little bit of relief involved, too. I wasn't sure I would ever properly get over his infidelity, so the fact he'd dumped me meant there was no going back. I was a bit embarrassed about having to tell the other Bluecoats I'd been dumped, but they were soon joking about me having my own star chart.

Needless to say, now I was single I did what every other 19-year-old girl does when she's away from home for the first time and surrounded by lads – I flirted my way through each and every day. I didn't sleep around but I became a massive party animal (minus the alcohol). While everyone was drinking wine and beer I'd have Slush Puppies instead, which meant that while they'd wake up in the morning feeling like death, I'd be as fresh as a daisy. Everyone else would be swaying around moaning about having to host a table tennis competition and I'd be skipping around feeling great. I used to swap shifts with people all the time because they felt too rough to do certain things. Looking back, I should have been paid a fortune in overtime!

I loved wearing my Pontins uniform – which usually consisted of shorts and a T-shirt or a tracksuit – and being able to perform all day. We could dance around being silly for hours on end and no one cared. It was all about entertaining the punters. I wasn't really the bingo-calling type or the one who would hang out with the old ladies. Whenever I did do bingo I used to put in loads of rude phrases like '69, dinner for two' or 'number three, going for a wee'. None of the old dears ever noticed but it kept me amused.

We used to take the guests out on these rambles and I always made sure I went along because there was a Maccy D's on the route. We'd take them to the beach and to visit all of these lovely old houses near the park, and then all of the guests would end up in the pub. The park bosses loved me going along because I was the only one who'd come back sober and in control, because while they were all downing pints I'd be in McDonald's.

I liked being with the children the most, making sure they were having the time of their lives. I'd play rounders and football and I'd take care of the kids' club. My nickname with them was Auntie Nut Nut, because I was always messing around and making them laugh. I was very maternal. I used to go down to their level and almost become a child myself. I loved working with kids, and so many of them would hang off me I looked like a bunch of grapes.

I was switched on from the moment I woke up until I went to bed and I used to get loads of fan mail because I put so much effort in. I could never have lunch by myself because we ate in the same restaurant as the guests, and all of the kids would come over and sit in my lap and want me to play with them. I never had a moment's rest. I also had to develop a very strong stomach to deal with all of the weeing and pooing of pants that went on. Only with the kids, I might add! I loved it all though. I felt like a bit of a mum to hundreds of kids throughout that time. Even if I had a day off, I used to go and hang out with the guests because I missed it so much.

In the evenings we had to dress up. I had to wear a blue skirt and jacket, a white shirt and a red cravat. I don't think it was my most stylish moment. We also had to wear bright red shoes as part of our outfit. They were a nightmare to find because there was no Internet back then, but I managed to track down some red patent ones in Bexleyheath that had a half heel and a rounded front. They were like a sensible granny shoe and were hideous. I'm not a heel person, but we had to dance with the guests wearing them and by the end of the night my ankles would be all swollen up like giant sausages.

We also had a team of people who would dress up as characters like Captain Crock, Florence the Ostrich, Chuckles the Cheeky Monkey, Zena the Zebra or Safari Sam. Over time they merged with the Bluecoats and we all started mucking in and dressing up as various animals. Because my middle name is Florence I always had to be Florence the Ostrich and I'd have to get up on stage and do these ridiculous dances. The costumes weren't washed that regularly, so if a smelly bloke had sweated in it the day before, the stink was shocking. When you're in a costume you're in it for a very long period of time, and you're not allowed to talk to the guests when you're wearing them because you have to keep an air of mystery! When the kids used to come up and speak to 'Florence', I wouldn't be able to say, 'Hello Billy' or 'Hello Jack' and wave like a lunatic. I used to find myself doing all of the silly smiling faces inside the costume anyway, even though the kids couldn't see me.

The character costumes weren't always used for their

correct purpose and there must be some very funny photos out there somewhere. All of the Bluecoats were constantly doing stupid things to make each other laugh and playing practical jokes. One of my closest friends was a girl called Emma. One night I was off work ill, so was in my chalet reading; you used to be able to get into people's chalets just by putting a knife into the gap in the door and catching the lock. Some of the other Bluecoats got into Emma's chalet and moved everything from inside and to exactly the same the same positions on the tarmac outside. Everyone found it hilarious, but when Emma came back to her chalet she screamed, burst into tears and ran back upstairs to tell our boss Graham Henry (who was also Shane Ritchie's boss when he worked there back in the day). Graham was furious and sacked loads of people on the spot. I managed to get away with it because he knew I wasn't involved, and everyone got reinstated the next day anyway. But that kind of sums up the kind of things that went on there.

I celebrated my 21st birthday while I was there and I decided to push the boat out and have some alcohol. I was drinking vodka Slush Puppies, something which resulted in me getting a tattoo of Thumper on my leg because I loved Bambi as a kid. I was going to have Po from the Teletubbies because they were really big at the time and I'm so relieved now that I didn't. I'd look ridiculous with a big red blob on my leg.

I trained to do all sorts of things at Pontins. I did circus training and used to have to balance on a pipe on a half-plank – something I definitely wouldn't have done if it hadn't been for my time there. My years there gave me so much confidence and it's where I learnt how to really work a crowd and deal with nerves. I also made some great friends that I'm still in touch with.

I would recommend working in a holiday camp to anyone who wants to get into performing as a career. As soon as you have that uniform on you can get away with acting as stupidly as you want. If you were to walk into a room not wearing a uniform and start dancing around, people would look at you like you're crazy. But the minute you had that blue coat on you were an entertainer.

We had loads of entertainers and bands that used to come in and perform and I used to really look up to them. We had hypnotists and puppeteers and all sorts. Bucks Fizz came to sing and I was so star-struck; we also had loads of touring bands who weren't famous but well known on the circuit. I always use to think it would be so amazing to be a part of something like that. Little did I know that later on down the line I would be.

One of the hypnotists was part of a theatre company and he heard me sing and asked me if I wanted to audition for something called *Sunday Night at the Palladium*. It was a variety show at The Palladium theatre in London, with loads of different songs from shows and performances from dance groups. I had to pay for my own costumes and sell a certain amount of tickets for it, but I decided it was still such a worthwhile thing to do.

We had rehearsals at Elstree Studios in Borehamwood where people from the BBC worked and *EastEnders* is filmed, so it felt very proper and I knew it would be an amazing experience to be involved in something so professional. In the end I got to open the show, singing 'Fame' and dressed in a gold two-tone suit my mum had bought me. It wasn't the most amazing show I'd ever been in but the theatre was packed and I felt like I was adding another string to my bow.

While I was rehearsing for the show I met a record producer called Danny Davies. He wanted me to record a song for a singer/songwriter competition he was entering. As always, I felt I had nothing to lose and it was going get me some more experience of being in a professional recording studio, which I was really looking forward to. I went down to the studio, which was in his house in Fulham, and recorded the track in a day. We got on really well and Danny said he wanted to carry on working with me.

The song ended up winning the competition and Danny gave me some of the prize money; I started recording a lot with him after that. He had songs he'd written that he needed someone to sing so he could showcase them. I'd travel up to London on my days off and record them. The songs got put into a library for TV shows or films and I'll never forget switching on *This Morning* one day to hear one of our songs playing in the background for their latest competition. I was stunned!

Danny was so professional that I could easily go into his studio, learn a song and record it in two hours. It was a real eye-opener for me, and such a good confidence builder. London is a bit of a closed door when it comes to session singers, and it's very hard to make connections and get on the first rung of the ladder, but he showed me a way to do it. Danny has since become a longstanding friend of mine and I still work with him to this day. He runs a company called Pirate Management and he definitely deserves a mention because he was a real inspiration to me early on. He's so good at what he does and I have masses of respect for him.

I'd had the time of my life being a Bluecoat but slowly things started to change. A lot of people left and the shows started being reinvented; I don't really like change so I found that hard to deal with. A lot of people came in from new camps and it wasn't the same anymore. I'd also lost so much weight from being on the go constantly and not having time to eat that I didn't look terribly well. I was also taking loads of ProPlus just to keep me awake because I didn't like taking breaks. When I did the Christmas season in 1998, which was to be my last, we had to be dressed as elves greeting people on the door of the restaurant at 7am and I didn't finish until 11 or 12 at night. I went down to about seven and a half to eight stone and I looked tiny.

As a result, I decided it was time for me to leave. I'd had

a great run but I was ready to go, so in early 1998 I headed home. I was sad to leave but I wasn't really gelling with all of the new people streaming in and I missed how it was before. I think when that happens you know your time is up. I wasn't thrilled at the thought of going back home to my warring parents, but I knew I had to start taking better care of myself, eating more and preparing for the next phase of my life – whatever that might be.

Back home nothing had moved on in any way. My dad was still a skinny shell of himself sitting on the sofa with a can of beer, and my mum was out working her balls off. I could definitely see where I got it from. My mum was so horrified by how slim I was when I walked in our front door that she cooked me a massive meal and sat there making sure I ate it. I could barely get it down because my stomach had shrunk so much as a result of skipping meals or eating sweets for dinner. I hadn't realised just how run-down I'd got and I needed that time back home to recuperate.

I soon settled back into a bit of a routine and it was nice to have all of my things around me again. I used to have serious issues with buying trainers when I was younger. Whenever I had money I used to go and buy a pair, so I had a big collection. I had these gold classic Reeboks, which were quite rare, but when I went to put them on one day I realised they were missing, along with a load of other pairs. I also noticed that my Chelsea FC manager's coat had disappeared, which was my pride and joy.

Later the same day I was walking up to the shop and I saw some young kid wearing *my* Reeboks. When I asked him where he'd got them from he replied, 'Your brother sold them to me.' I was furious! I kept seeing kids around the estate wearing my clothes and shoes and I could have killed my brothers. I try to be understanding about it now because they were obviously desperate for cash, even if it was just to buy weed, but at the time I was gutted.

I got a bit down being back home because it wasn't exactly *fun*, but my mum kept me going. I couldn't sign on because I'd resigned from my job, but I was confident enough that I would get myself another one. Soon enough I got a job doing market research again and I started hanging around with an old friend of mine, Julie Bushell, who is the daughter of the journalist Garry Bushell. At that time Garry was doing a TV show called *Bushell On The Box*, which was filmed in his front room. I used to love going around there because sometimes famous people would come round to film the show and Julie and I would always sneak downstairs and try to catch a glimpse of them. I answered their house phone once and it was Dale Winton; I was so bloody excited!

My dream was still to sing, so I started going to auditions at places like Pineapple Dance Studios in Covent Garden or Danceworks, which was just off Oxford Street. They were always holding auditions for something or other and I used to go along for fun, clutching my trusty CD of backing tracks. Sometimes I didn't even know what I was auditioning for –

it could have been a pole-dancing club in Timbuktu – but I'd go to get experience and get used to being knocked back. I wanted to become strong and resilient and learn not to let the disappointments get me down. That way, I figured, when something I really *did* want came up I could go along and not be afraid of being told 'no'. I know it sounds mad but for some reason the knockbacks gave me more confidence and I wanted to be able to walk into a room and give off the impression that I felt like I deserved to be there.

I went for an audition for a Disney Cruise Liner once and there were all of these people there who looked like Pocahontas with long dark hair, or Prince Charming with a big blonde flick. I arrived in jeans and hoodie and as I got nearer to the front I panicked because I didn't look like *anyone* from a Disney movie. Princess Chav, maybe? My group got called in and I thought about edging my way out and doing a runner, but it was so busy there was no way I could go anywhere *but* the audition room. They must have wondered what the hell I was doing there. I looked like someone's weird sister who had come along for a laugh. Funnily enough I didn't get offered the role of Princess Jasmine.

One day Julie told she was going for an audition to be an entertainer on a Thompson cruise ship, and asked me if I'd go with her. I had trials for a woman's football team at the Arsenal training ground on the same day, so I was really torn. I still loved football and I'd never stopped playing, but I didn't enjoy it *quite* as much as I enjoyed singing. I thought about it long and hard and decided that I could go and try out for the football team anytime, but the cruise ship sounded like a great opportunity. Also because I wasn't *desperate* for the job, I knew I wasn't going to be a shaking mess and I'd probably end up having quite a laugh.

The auditions were being held at Danceworks and when Julie and I arrived there were hundreds of people waiting to be seen. We were all waiting in the restaurant area and we could hear everyone else auditioning. I started talking to some of the other hopefuls and because we were waiting around for so long I went into full on Bluecoat mode and started telling jokes and doing Frank Spencer impressions. I was pretty cocky and I was making everyone laugh by basically being a bit of a show-off.

When my name was called I suddenly found myself feeling quite nervous. Maybe I did really want the job after all? I sang a Mariah Carey song – although for the life of me I can't remember which one – and afterwards I went back to the restaurant where we all waited to hear if we'd got through to the next stage or not. I was so happy when my name was called, but also slightly terrified because we were expected to dance in the second round, and following routines really wasn't my strong point. I can put my leg behind my head, which I'm quite proud of, but I'm not sure that's a good skill to have on a posh cruise ship!

I wasn't the world's *worst* dancer back then, but I had no

professional experience (unless you call dancing around in an ostrich suit professional experience?). There were girls there in leotards and legwarmers doing the splits to warm up, and I was wearing one of my football tracksuits and trainers looking like I was planning on running a marathon.

I went into the audition room feeling like such a fool. These gorgeous girls were pirouetting around me, and being a footballer I wasn't the most graceful person in the world. We were shown a dance routine and we all had to keep up with the instructor. I was going the wrong way and getting the moves completely wrong and in my head I was thinking, 'Never mind. I've got all of my football gear with me. Maybe I can still make the trials at Arsenal?'

I was convinced I wasn't going to get through that round. When they asked me to stay for another interview I was so astonished I blurted out, 'Are you sure? *Me*?!' It turned out that two of the people I'd been telling jokes to in the restaurant worked for Thompson recruitment and they'd been watching everyone to see if people were being entertaining. They said I really stood out as someone who was a laugh and really friendly. Result.

I had to have an interview with several Thompson execs and when they asked me what my strengths were I replied, 'I've been a Bluecoat and I'm really good at talking to people from all different walks of life. I'm not a topper (someone who's always trying to be better than other people) and I'm really easy going. I also know how to make people feel special and I'm always up for a laugh.' The interview seemed to go well but we weren't going to hear for a minimum of two weeks, so we were sent away with all of the information about what the job would entail and told to be patient. The more I read about where we'd get to go and what we'd get to do, the more I thought 'Wow, I could really do this. It would be amazing. I want this job!'

I couldn't stop thinking about the job and every day I wanted it more and more. I've always been a bit impatient, so I decided to take matters into my own hands. I rang up Thompson recruitment and said in the stupidly strong cockney accent I had at the time, 'Hello, I was at the auditions last week and…' Before I could even finish the sentence the woman on the other end said, 'Is that Sam? We were just talking about you.' Out of all of the hundreds of people who had auditioned that day she'd recognised me. I could only think that was a good thing? I wanted to shout, 'Please tell me you want me!' There was a pause and then she said, 'I shouldn't really be telling you this but you've got the job. Congratulations. We'll be sending all of your documentation to you soon.'

I got off the phone and immediately said to my dad, 'I'm going to the Mediterranean. I've got the bloody job!' I was thrilled but also scared because I was 22 and I was going to be going abroad on my own for the first time ever. But what did I have to lose? I had nothing to keep me at home and I was desperate for some adventure. About a week later this huge folder arrived telling me exactly where I was going, who I would be working with, what I would be expected to do and which songs I'd be singing. There were seven CDs from various shows that we'd be performing and I had to learn all of the lyrics beforehand. I also had to have a full medical, including a smear test, which I'd never had before.

I travelled up to Wakefield to do rehearsals for the shows with all of the other staff members. We learnt dance routines and we had to be able to perform together flawlessly. The entertainment team was made up of three female singers, including me, three male singers and four female dancers. One of the other singers, Jolene, was from the same area as me and we got on really well. The other female singer, Sarah, was amazing but she was much more of a musical theatre singer so she had really precise diction, which sounded a bit strange when she was singing pop songs. She put so much effort into everything she did and has since landed a role in a West End show, which she totally deserves. I'm so happy for her.

As for the men: John was a total lad and now performs in a Gary Barlow tribute act, Richard is an events manager and also does musical theatre, and Andrew is an absolutely wonderful guy who's still singing now and does a lot of great charity work. The four dancers were called Hayley, Shirley, Carla and Nicola and we all bonded really quickly. We used to rehearse all day and then go down the local pub and do karaoke in the evenings. We were a bit of a powerhouse when we walked through the door and no one else got much of a chance to get on the mic when we were around.

All of the crew I worked with came along to the *The X Factor* tour and we had a big reunion, which was brilliant but surreal. Some of us hadn't seen each other for 14 years and now we're all married and we've got kids. I still think of myself as that young girl in some ways, and I think it's a real eye opener when you see old friends all grown up and settled down. I think I still expected some of them to look like they were in their early twenties, as if they'd been stuck in a time warp.

While I was in Wakefield I got the results of my medical, including the outcome of my smear test. I will never, ever forget looking down at the letter and seeing the words 'severe cancer cells' written down and then 'abnormal cells' written in the first line. Nowadays the word cancer isn't used – doctors say 'mild, moderate or severe changes' instead – and you can imagine my reaction. I was petrified. No one in my family had ever had cancer, so it wasn't something I was familiar with. But of course I'd heard enough stories to know that the disease can be fatal and it frightened the living shit out of me.

I went straight to a doctor who explained everything to me and said I would need the bad cells removed from my cervix. The waiting list for the procedure was three months and I had to be on the ship in two months' time, so I ended up paying almost £500 to get it done privately at Queen

Mary's Hospital in Sidcup. In the end, I had it the day I was leaving for my first ever cruise, which was far from ideal. I was in hospital in the morning and in the afternoon I had to fly out to the dry dock in Malaga. I was in a lot of pain but the excitement of what lay ahead helped to take my mind off of it.

CHAPTER 5

COME SAIL AWAY

As soon as I arrived in Malaga in March 1999 it was go go go. We had to go through all of the choreography again and I was still in agony from the procedure. I was bleeding a lot and the pain lasted for a couple of weeks. I don't think dancing around was the best thing I could have done, but thank goodness for that medical because if I hadn't had that test done I would never have known I had a problem.

We were all so excited about finally getting on to the ship and I couldn't wait to see where I was going to be living for the next few months. When we boarded, everything was covered in plastic and it smelled so fresh and new. I had a suitcase full of glamorous dresses that I'd borrowed from anyone and everyone to get me through the first few weeks. During the day we wore a Thompson T-shirt and shorts, but we had to look smart in the evenings, especially when we attended things like the Captain's Dinner. I don't do dresses so I had to beg, borrow and steal enough outfits to tide me over until I could afford to top up my wardrobe. I was a tomboy who struggled to put make-up on, so to suddenly have to wear floor-length gowns, glitzy jewellery and have my hair in a chignon felt so alien. I was so shoddy with everything; I didn't have a clue! All I wanted was to go on stage and sing for people but the whole look was a massive part of it. It wasn't even like my make-up could be subtle. I had to wear white and black eye shadow, bright red lipstick and false eyelashes. I felt like a clown.

A lot of people found themselves feeling really ill for the first few days on the ship, just because they weren't used to bobbing up and down. It's easy to underestimate how sick and disoriented it can make you feel if you haven't done it before. I saw several of the crew rushing to the toilet at various times or gripping onto the bannisters for dear life when they were walking down the stairs. For some reason I was really lucky, and took to it like a duck to water, if you'll pardon the pun. I find the sea quite soothing, especially when going to sleep. It was daunting at times because it was the first time I'd been somewhere where I couldn't just hop into a car and go home, but the sight of the sun and beautiful new countries soon helped me get over that!

We'd been taught all of these skills in the run-up to the guests coming on board, like crowd management and how to sympathise with people by putting your head to one side.

We also used the word 'excellent' with people constantly, with the idea that when they came to fill out their comment forms at the end of the week they'd been so used to hearing the word they'd be more inclined to tick the 'excellent' box. Nine times out of ten I was excellent anyway, though!

We travelled to so many places like Gibraltar, Cádiz, Lisbon, all around the Greek islands and Italy. I ended up buying a Spanish mobile so that every time we were in Spanish waters I could phone home cheaply. My mum and I set up a joint bank account into which all of my payments went so she could look after it for me. Drinks on the ship were half-price for us and I didn't have to buy any food because it was all provided, so I was able to save quite a lot of money. The only problem was I didn't like a lot of the food on the ship because it was too rich for me. Yes, the fussy eater in me reared its head again. Things like stuffed aubergines or moussaka didn't appeal at all, so if that was what we were given for dinner, mostly I would go without. We weren't allowed to have food in our cabins, so it wasn't like I could nip back there and eat something else.

I became quite ill for a while because much like at Pontins, I was running around constantly and not eating properly. I was also smoking a lot so lost loads of weight really quickly. At one point I collapsed and had to be put on a drip. After that happened, whenever we docked I was allowed to go and buy tins of ravioli and other things I liked and keep a stash of them hidden away. While the rest of the staff were tucking into all these fancy dishes I was taking tins of spaghetti to the staff mess so the chefs could warm them up for me.

The staff piss-ups on the boat were legendary, but apart from the odd few B52 cocktails I was pretty well behaved. There was only one time I got properly drunk by mistake. Never again, etc. One night there was a problem with the lights on the ship because of an electrical fault and that meant we couldn't leave the port in Malaga. We had to stay over, so a load of us went out to this bar. I was drinking vodka and orange and because Spanish measures are absolutely ridiculous I got drunk really, *really* quickly. I can still taste it in the back of my throat now and it makes me heave. We didn't have a curfew that night, so we headed back to the ship at around 2am, and as soon as the fresh air hit me I was gone. I was so hammered I had to be held up by other members of staff.

When we got back to the ship the captain was stood at the top of the walkway looking furious. Everyone was shouting at me to stand up because I was dragging my feet along but I was well and truly hammered. I climbed up the gangway and started singing to him, which is *not* something you do to the captain of the ship: you're supposed to have the utmost respect for him. He could easily have sacked me but according to one of my friends he had a bit of a smile on his face, and instead of bollocking me he told my friends to take me the back way to my cabin to keep me out of sight of any passengers. As soon as I got into my cabin I was violently sick, and I carried on throwing up for most of the night, which meant I got zero sleep.

I woke up the next morning with a crashing hangover and a massive sense of shame. I'd been kicked in the face when I was 14 playing football and lost one of my teeth. As a result I had a plate with a false tooth attached that I could take in and out. When I eventually managed to haul myself up and look in the mirror I realised that my false tooth was missing. I looked everywhere for it and then it hit me that I must have flushed it down the toilet when I was being sick. I went into full-on panic mode. I had to perform that night and I had this massive hole where my tooth should have been. Every time I spoke I was whistling through the gap and I was mortified.

Everyone was taking the mickey out of me and singing 'Whistle While You Work'. Every time I talked to someone I was covering my mouth. But 'the show must go on', and that night I had to get up on stage in front of a packed room of people and sing 'Big Spender', which actually sounded more like Big Ssshhhpender.

Thankfully we stayed moored in Malaga for another day and somehow my friend Janice managed to get me an appointment with a dentist the next morning. I had an impression done and I was able to pick up my new tooth before we set sail again. What a relief. Funnily enough that was the last time I tested whether or not I liked get really drunk, whether by mistake or otherwise. I didn't.

At the end of every month we'd all get our bar bills and sit around guessing whose was the highest and the lowest. I used to buy other people alcohol sometimes, but I stuck to Fanta after that fateful night, so mine was always the lowest at around £40-£50. Some people's were £400–£500, which was about a quarter of their wages. And the drinks were half-price as well! Most of my spare money went on CDs and DVDs. I was a fan of the New Radicals and Jamiroquai. 'You Get What You Give' was my song at that time. We used to take it in turns to DJ in the staff mess, but some people used to play shit music on purpose because they knew I'd get annoyed and take over, meaning they could go and sit in the bar and get drunk.

A few months after I started on the ship I paid for my mum and her friend to come out and visit me. Sadly my dad was too unwell to come but I think it was exactly what Mum needed and deserved after all her hard work. To be fair it probably felt like a holiday for my dad too, because it meant no arguments for a week and he could have his drinking buddies round without being told off!

Mum and her mate got upgraded and I gave the bar staff loads of pre-paid slips for drinks, so they had a whale of a time. We did two shows a night and Mum always tried to sneak in and see me perform twice because she was so proud of me. Before she left the boat at the end of the trip, Mum went to settle her bar bill. The woman in front of her had spent £700; my mum's was £5.40 for the entire trip. On the other hand, not surprisingly my bar bill that week was the biggest it would be the whole time I was working on the ships.

Mum loved her time on board so much I paid for her to came back with my nan a few months later. Because my nan was old she used to wash her knickers every night and hang them up in her cabin, so you could often tell where her room was if they were billowing around on the balcony. She also had a bit of a crush on the Spanish doctor, so she used to feign illness just so she could go and visit him. It was brilliant having family coming to see me because I did get homesick sometimes. I missed stupid things like my own bed and certain chocolate bars, but I never once regretted going.

Although I had an amazing time on the ship, I also experienced one of the scariest moments of my life while I was there. One night Jolene and I were sat outside in an area called the Winter Gardens having a cigarette before the evening performance. We were leaving Morocco and we both noticed that the sea seemed really choppy. Suddenly this massive wave leapt over the side of the ship and completely soaked us both. Jolene went one way and I went the other and when we scrambled back onto our seats we were thinking 'What the hell just happened?' My show make-up was running down my face and my hair was dripping. The further we went out to sea the worse the wind became, but by then it was too late for us to turn around and go back to land.

When we went back inside the ship was rocking all over the place and plates and glasses were slipping off tables and smashing. Of course we had to try and keep people calm and act normally, so we went ahead with the entertainment. The only problem was I was scheduled to sing 'My Heart Will Go On' from *Titanic*, which probably wasn't the most appropriate song to be singing when the waves were crashing against the side of the boat and the guests were panicking. We couldn't even change the running order of the songs because the backing tracks were all on one CD and it was impossible to skip through them. I had no choice but to get up and perform the most ill-timed song of my career.

Just before I took to the stage the casino table fell on some poor woman's leg and the grand piano slid across the room. There was broken glass everywhere and people were going back to their cabins and putting on life jackets, then coming back to watch the show wearing them. One little kid even came up and asked me if we were going to die. I told him that it was all just a silly game, but I was feeling really breathless.

I was begging the cruise director not to make me sing because I was struggling to stand up, but five minutes later I found myself out on stage with a painted-on smile preparing to do my best Celine Dion impersonation. I had to hold on to a stool and stand with my legs as wide apart as I could to balance myself. As soon as the backing track started the looks on people's faces were priceless. Some found it funny; others were horrified. I felt so guilty but I was just doing what I'd been told.

The Captain was amazing. He was walking around calmly trying to reassure everyone, but I genuinely feared for my life. Parts of the ship were flooded, people were throwing up and I was physically shaking with fear. I vowed there and then that I would never sing 'My Heart Will Go On' again – and I didn't until I performed it on *The X Factor*. People had asked me so many times since that night to sing it when I'd done shows or karaoke, but I'd flatly refused. Thankfully, by the next day the weather had calmed down, although the clean-up operation was quite something. It's a night I'll remember in great detail for the rest of my life.

Towards the end of my first season, I heard about some openings on another ship called *The Emerald*. The cruise was called The Millennium Cruise and it was travelling all around the Caribbean and docking in New Orleans on Millennium night. Anyone on our ship who wanted to try out for a job was allowed to audition. If we got accepted we'd have to put in extra time while doing all of our other work because there were four new shows to learn, but I was willing to put in the hard work. It sounded like too good an opportunity to miss. Quite a few people from the entertainment crew auditioned and thankfully most of us, including me, were accepted. We went straight into rehearsals and although it was bloody hard work I knew that it would all be worth it when we moored up in sunny St Lucia.

I was supposed to have a two-week break back home in Kent before I joined *The Emerald*, only unbeknown to me all of Darren's family had booked a trip to come and see me as a surprise. I felt terrible that I wouldn't be there, so I asked my boss if I could stay on the ship and pay as a passenger. Instead he said I could stay for free if I did two cabaret performances, which sounded like a great deal to me! We had an amazing time together and it was the perfect way to round off my first ever job on a cruise ship.

After that everything was a bit of a rush. I got the chance to go home for a few days and then I had to go straight to Manchester to do more rehearsals. I flew direct from Manchester to the Dominican Republic and it was a totally different ball game to the last cruise. This was big time.

The ship was in dry dock and even though we were living on the ship from day one we got to go out and explore. One night we all went out to a nightclub called Mambo's. When we got there the club was on the beach and it was totally open air. At one point I was dancing away to 'YMCA' and having such a laugh. I looked around me and thought, 'My god, I'm being paid to be here. It doesn't get much better than this!'

I wish now I'd written a diary about all of the sights I saw on that ship. It was unbelievable. I went to the Dunn's River Falls in Jamaica, and the rainforest and places I could only ever have dreamed of seeing. One of the best things for me was when we landed in Barbados. I went to the nearest phone box and I called my dad and said, 'Dad, I'm ringing you from Barbados!' He laughed and said, 'Alright, you win.' It was one of those brilliant, life-affirming moments, one that I'll never forget.

Romance-wise, I was always very careful not to get involved with any of the guests when I worked on the liners because I knew that they'd soon be gone again and I didn't want to get hurt. I did go on a few dates with a Greek guy who worked on the ship. He was nice enough but the language barrier proved to be a bit of a problem and it fizzled out. I didn't mind too much because I was having so much fun and I was perfectly happy on my own. The only guy I got involved with was called Andrew who was a brain surgeon. He was lovely, but I was intimidated by him because he'd been to St Andrews University and I felt as common as muck compared to him and always worried about saying the wrong thing. We spent quite a lot of time together but I knew it couldn't go anywhere. I would never have felt good enough for him.

New Year's Eve 1999 was one of the most incredible nights of my life. We cruised down the Panama Canal into New Orleans and it felt like one of the most glamorous – if not *the* most glamorous – things that had ever happened to me.

Someone had to stay on the ship and DJ for all of the guests that night, but because we were going to be docked, all of the entertainment crew wanted to go out and have a great time in New Orleans, not be stuck on the boat playing

Prince's '1999'. We were going to pull names out of a hat, but in the end I had a long hard think about how I could benefit from it. I went and spoke to the cruise director and told him I was willing to nominate myself if I could get the next day off to go sightseeing. We weren't leaving the dock until the evening, so I would have plenty of time to look around.

We did a show earlier in the evening but I got to see the fireworks at midnight before I had to run downstairs to the disco and start DJ'ing. There must have been about ten people left on the entire ship but someone had to play music for them! I only ended up playing for about an hour before everyone went to bed and then I headed off the boat to meet some of my friends. The party atmosphere on the streets of New Orleans was incredible and I had an amazing night. And while everyone else was hungover and working the next day, I felt fine and I got to have a whole day of sightseeing.

On the flip side there was a very sad moment on *The Emerald* when one gentleman died of old age the first day he arrived on the ship. When we docked he was going to be taken off the ship and it was the entertainment crew's job to distract everyone so they didn't see him being wheeled off on a trolley underneath a black sheet. It was funny and tragic at the same time because there was a lot of tap dancing and jazz hands involved as we frantically did everything in our power to make sure no one noticed what was going on.

I was also in charge of 'Singles Mingles' on the ship, when all of the single people would get together. I'd introduce them to each other to break the ice and they'd all sit together on the singles' table that night. By the end of the cruise they'd be having a whale of a time and I had quite a good couple success rate. There were two weddings as a result of introductions we did on that cruise, so I felt like I was the Cilla of the waves!

One day around March time I was walking past the kids' club and I could see that the women in charge was having a bit of a nightmare. I'd almost finished work for the day so I went in and offered to give her a hand. I felt like I was back to being a Bluecoat again. I got so engrossed in helping her I completely forgot I was supposed to be doing a deck tour with some of the guests. Luckily someone covered it for me, but when the cruise director found out he came storming into the kids' club and frogmarched me to his office. He was always much tougher on the women than the men and he started shouting at me saying, 'You think you're this and that and I'm telling you now you're not.' I knew that other staff members would have heard every word because he was bellowing so loudly and I got so upset I started to cry. He spoke to me like I was about six years old and when I left I was so angry and embarrassed I went straight down to my cell and I wrote on a piece of paper 'I wish to resign from this ship' and I put it in his pigeonhole.

A while later I was in the theatre rehearsing for that evening's show with the rest of the entertainment crew when the cruise director walked in with a face like thunder. He announced to everyone that I'd resigned. I hadn't told any of them and the last thing I wanted was my friends hearing it from him. He told me I had until the end of the day to make up my mind and then he turned on his heel and stomped out again.

I'd had an amazing time on the ship until that point, but I was really starting to miss home. I took some time to think about it and after weighing up the pros and cons I decided that I was ready to leave. I told the cruise director about my decision and the next thing I knew his bosses had flown out to beg me to stay. But my mind was made up. It turned out I'd been sent a lot of fan mail (although I hadn't actually got to see any of it, for some reason) and I'd had brilliant feedback so Thompson were desperate to keep me on. I'd gelled with so many guests and a lot had got in touch with the company to say I'd made their holiday. I was told that if I resigned I would never be able to work for Thompson cruises again, but that didn't deter me. I'd loved my fantasy life hopping from country to country, but now it was time to get back to real life.

I knew I would miss the cruise and all of my friends and although going home felt like the right thing to do, when it came to saying goodbye it was so hard. I was sobbing when I got on the coach to go to the airport. One of the other entertainers, Andrew Holt, had got me really into Barry Manilow, and I listened to his Greatest Hits album for the entire journey to try and take my mind off leaving everyone.

My brother picked me up from Gatwick airport and

drove me home. The first couple of days were brilliant. It was great to catch up with family and friends and sleep in my childhood bedroom again. It felt like I'd been away for ages. But that initial buzz didn't last long and my parents' arguing soon started to get to me again. My dad was sat on the sofa wetting himself, my mum was out working her backside off, and although my life had changed because of the experiences I'd had, nothing else had. Mum spoke to me about leaving my dad again and I knew without a doubt they would be better off apart, but they had to think about the logistics. Where would they both live? How could they afford two separate homes? Sadly, them not splitting up was down to money, and nothing else.

CHAPTER 6

THE SHOW MUST GO ON

As usual I hadn't really put much thought into what I was going to do work-wise once I got back home. But – surprise surprise! – my mum came to my rescue and got me some work doing market research with her again. It was definitely one of those jobs you could dip in and out of, so it was perfect for the nomadic life I had back then.

The work was steady and relatively easy, but I soon started to miss singing terribly. I heard about a bar up in London called Singers that had an open mic night so I decided to go. An artist called Jocelyn Brown was the compère and you put your name down and then waited your turn. I sang a gospel song and afterwards was approached by a guy who introduced himself as Roachie and told me he was a talent scout. I didn't know anything about that kind of thing at the time, but he said he wanted to introduce me to someone at Sanctuary Records, which is the same record label as Iron Maiden. We arranged to meet up a few days later at the Sanctuary café; I ended up sitting next to Roger Daltrey and I was properly freaked out. He was eating beans on toast and he seemed really laid back. I desperately wanted to say something to him, but I was worried that if I opened my mouth I'd start singing him songs from the film *Tommy* or something.

Roachie came and met me and took me down to the R&B department where I met up with a record executive, whose name I can't remember. He said he really liked me but that he wanted my image to develop before they would do anything with me. They wanted to totally change my image. I wasn't sure about it at all but Roachie convinced me to at least see what plans they had for me before I decided whether to go ahead.

We met again the following day and he took me into a studio where these two really cool girls were dancing. It was the girls' job to try and teach me how to move like them because the record company wanted me to be more 'street'. It truly wasn't me at all and as soon as I got the chance I scarpered. If they didn't want me for me they couldn't have me at all. I didn't want to be a fraud and change the way I walked, talked and danced; I felt really uncomfortable with it. This was in the days before everyone had mobile phones and I didn't have one at the time, so the exec had no way of getting hold of me. I've never heard from him again, and I can't say I'm all that surprised after doing a runner!

A short while after that I got a phone call from Graham Henry, my old manager at Pontins, asking me if I'd go back and perform at Pakefield in exchange for a week's free holiday. I jumped at the chance – a free holiday and I got to sing? It was a no-brainer.

I was on the same bill as a travelling cabaret act called The Tony Carnagie Show. They played at loads of different venues around the country and they were really well respected. Tony was a bit of a legend because he used to dress up as famous divas like Judy Garland, Tina Turner and Cher, and people used to travel for miles to come and see him. He also had other singers on his roster who performed charts hits and show tunes, and at the time he was working with a woman called Julie, who really stood out to me because she had a really powerful voice.

After I'd performed a medley of songs, Tony approached me and asked if I wanted to audition for his show. He explained they were based in Leicester, so it would mean moving up there permanently, but I didn't care one bit. I always thought the travelling acts that performed at Pontins were awesome and I wanted it to be the next step for me, so it was perfect timing. It was effectively a full-time job, only we would be working in the evenings rather than during the day, which I was used to anyway. I didn't plan to work in market research for the rest of my life and if I joined the band I would be making money doing what I loved again.

About a week later, I travelled to Leicester to audition.

Tony didn't tell me outright that I had the job, but afterwards he took me to a few shops in the town centre to try on some outfits he thought would work well in the show, which was a bit of a giveaway. When he did finally break the news that he wanted me to join the band, I didn't hesitate to say yes, even though it meant moving somewhere I only knew one person I'd met twice before!

Tony and his boyfriend Gary came and picked me up from Kent in late July 2000. They rented me a room in their house and Tony used to take a certain amount out of my wages each month to cover food and bills. He became like a second mum to me because he did all of my washing and cooked my dinner every night. He knew I hated parsnips, so it became a running joke that he would cut them in the shape of potatoes and sneak them on to my plate. I felt right at home and we were really comfortable in each other's company. If ever I was homesick he would do silly things to make me laugh. I always had chocolate in my room and Tony would sneak in, eat it and then put the wrapper on the floor and pretend their dogs Poppy and Chaz had eaten it.

Tony and I were so mischievous together. We spent that first summer sunbathing and having a right laugh. He had a loft full of costumes, from sequined dresses to wigs. We used to get really dressed up and then sit out the front of the house in garden chairs and watch people do a double-take as they drove past. One time a small fire broke out in the park out the back of the house, so we had to ring the fire brigade. While we waited for them to arrive I ran upstairs and put on a sequined bikini and the wig I wore when I performed songs from *Miss Saigon*. I was still really slim then and I climbed up onto the shed. When the fireman arrived I shouted, 'Help, help!' This very handsome fireman turned around and blasted me with water and Tony and I were in stitches.

Sadly, after a lot of unhappy years together, in 2001 my parents finally decided to split up for good. I knew it was the best thing for both of them and all I could do was be there to support them. My mum moved out to another place nearby and she later started seeing one of my brother Charlie's friends, Ray, which I was totally fine with. I wasn't heartbroken because I saw it coming and I just wanted them both to be as happy as they could be. My dad was living on his own in our old house and his mum, my nan, was going round every day to look after him and take him meals because he still couldn't get around very well.

I still used to go back home to see my family quite often, so I spent a lot of time going to and from Leicester on National Express coaches. When I went home after one visit to Kent, Tony and Gary had moved all of my stuff into another, bigger, room. They'd got me a lovely new bed and even put chocolates on my pillow. It was so sweet and I have nothing but fond memories of living with them.

We were so close we even holidayed together, and in 2001

Tony, Gary, Tony's nephew and niece and I all headed to Florida for some fun. We flew out on 10th September and headed straight to Disney World on the 11th. We were on the *Jaws* ride when all of a sudden people started running around the park screaming. We had no idea what was going on and it was only when they stopped the ride and got everyone off that one of the Disney staff members told us that a plane had flown into one of the Twin Towers. Everyone was evacuated from the park immediately. There was still a plane in the sky and they thought it was heading in the direction of the coast of Florida, so they didn't want to take any chances. We were all told to go back to our hotels and stay inside. We all went to Tony and Gary's room and I'll never forget us all sitting there in a state of total shock watching the second plane hit the other Twin Tower. It didn't feel real and it still doesn't now. It was like watching the worst movie imaginable and I was in floods of tears thinking about all of those poor people who were involved. My mum was frantically calling to make sure we were all okay and I don't think any of us said more than two words to each other all day. We all sat there glued to the TV not believing what we were seeing. Not surprisingly all of the parks stayed closed all week and the airport only opened up again the day we were due to fly home because everywhere was on such high alert. I still can't believe it happened.

I had such a lovely time living with Tony and Gary

but after a couple of years I decided I needed some more independence, so I found a flat to rent above a shop just around the corner. I moved in with a girl called Melissa and one of the other girls who had joined the band, Ellie. It worked out at £120 a month each for rent and then bills on top, which doesn't sound like a fortune but I wasn't exactly coining it in. I pretty much lived off pasta and chips from the chippie below us the entire time I was there. We all got on really well and as you can imagine we weren't always that well behaved. We lived opposite a taxi firm and the girls always used to dare me to flash my boobs at the drivers for a giggle. I've never been able to resist a dare. I just hope there isn't any photographic evidence anywhere…

The band didn't usually have any gigs from Monday to Thursday, but at weekends we got bookings all around the country. Every Friday everyone would descend on Tony's house, then we'd all pile into his van with the equipment and costumes and off we'd go. Sometimes we were given a caravan at a venue where we could stay overnight, and even though I didn't drink we always had a bloody good laugh. When we performed at holiday camps I used to look at the Red- or Bluecoats or Haven Mates and think 'that used to be me', and I felt so proud that I'd ended up exactly where I wanted to.

We took our jobs as entertainers really seriously but we also had fun if we knew the audience were up for it. We used to do silly things like put a mic stand behind someone so they fell over, or one of us would mute someone else's mic and sing their line for them in a silly voice.

The best audiences were the ones you could have a laugh with. I used to go up to bald blokes and say, 'Awww, it's such a shame. He spent ages doing his hair tonight and he's come out without it.' Or I'd go and sit on a guy's lap and start stroking his hair, and then pretend to wipe the grease off on his top. If the audience were up for it, it made the night so much more enjoyable. It was such a fun time.

We'd wear really smart clothes at the beginning of the show and people would think we were a really straightforward band. Then Tony would disappear and come back dressed as Tina Turner. Everyone would assume he was a female tribute act and some of the guys would be leering at him because he had the most incredible body. The looks on their faces when they realised it was actually a man were priceless. I used to love the element of surprise, the moment when the realisation kicked in and everyone's jaws dropped. Tony would also come on as Cher in an outfit that consisted of a black sequined leotard with false boobs. He'd tuck his willy under so he had a beetle bonnet, and he wore this huge wig. He'd burst into 'If I Could Turn Back Time' and he was so good people thought he was singing over a backing track, but he didn't mime once. He was incredible.

I became one of the longest-standing female singers in the show. A lot of people came and went but the show pretty much always stayed the same. My main job was to act out scenes from *Miss Saigon* and *Chicago*, during which I had to make out I was drunk. I even pretended to play the trumpet on one track. The first half of the show was proper cabaret, and the second half consisted of songs that people could get up and dance to. We had a section called Pop Goes The 80s, which was packed full of tracks by people like Soft Cell and Madonna, and that always got people up on their feet. Especially after a few wines. We used to get people trying to get up on stage and join in and all sorts. We never knew what to expect.

Our bread and butter work, as we called it, was the social clubs. If there was bingo on you daren't even speak let alone sing, but as soon as that was finished we'd get up and do our turn. There were probably only a handful of clubs that were well behaved and appreciated a good singer, but when you got a good one it made all the difference.

If there was another game of bingo on after you, the crowd were pretty much waiting for us to get off the stage so they could play again. They had very little interest in what we were doing; they just wanted to try and win some money. Our routine generally went like this: turn up at 6.30pm, watch a game of bingo, perform, watch more bingo (and possibly a meat raffle), then perform again. Our first performance was always the toilet/fag break because people hadn't dared to move during the game, but the second performance wasn't as bad because people would be well lubricated by then. They still talked all the way through but were also a bit more up for watching a show. It was almost like clockwork every time we performed. The audience would be chatting away, then I'd do a high note at the end of the show, they'd all stop and clap and cheer, and then they'd turn to each other and carry on chatting. It was the same in a lot of clubs we went to. We'd always round off the evening with a real belter of a track, and the second we finished the crowd would start shouting for more. I used to stand on stage thinking, 'More? You didn't even watch us!'

We used to do a lot of charity gigs as well, and we performed alongside the likes of Jane McDonald, Ray Quinn and Beverley Knight. I really looked up to Jane because she's a singer's singer. She had been on the cruise ships so she'd come from where I'd come from and she'd carved out this amazing career for herself. I remember being gutted when we performed on the same night as her because I had a throat infection and my voice wasn't what it should have been. I met her beforehand and I said I wasn't feeling well, so she stood in the wings rooting me on. She gave me a huge hug afterwards and I was so taken aback. I was only in my mid-20s and she was a real idol to me.

I performed for Sir Alex Ferguson and Ricky Hatton at one charity event, and I was properly star-struck. Ricky and I had a photo taken where we hammed it up and pretended to have a bit of a spar and my brothers were well impressed. I always used to chat to the celebs because I found that world fascinating. We did one charity concert for Destination Florida, which does amazing work sending terminally ill children out to Florida for holidays. Ray Quinn also performed, but I'd never watched *Brookside* so I didn't know who he was. He was this tiny, lovely looking kid with a brilliant voice, only 17, and he'd just got through to the Bootcamp stage of *The X Factor*. He wasn't supposed to tell anyone, but he let it slip and I knew he'd go a long way because he was such a great guy and so talented. In fact, he was so good someone offered to donate £1,000 to charity if he sang another song once he'd finished his set.

I won't lie and say much of it was glamorous. If we got a dressing room we felt lucky. I've got changed in caravans, toilets, the back of the van – you name it. If we did get a changing room they were rarely clean and often didn't have a toilet or running water. If you were in the room the night after a stripper had performed you'd find banana skins and dirty thongs and all sorts stuck to the carpet. There are only a handful of clubs that have got it properly sorted when it comes to dressing rooms, and performing in some really lovely places since *The X Factor* really opens your eyes to how nice they can be with even just a little bit of effort.

I'm not the demanding type and I don't expect a lavish rider (the food and drink you can request for your dressing room) or anything, but even just having somewhere to sit down and make a cup of tea makes a massive difference. Performing at G-A-Y in London is always a real treat because you get so spoilt. The owner Jeremy Joseph has got it so right. There are massive tubs of sweets and a fridge full of drinks and it's heaven. Even now when I perform live I only ever ask for tea, a kettle and milk, and half the time I take my own Tetley with me because I like a nice strong brew. If I can get sandwiches for the crew as well then it's a bonus because hungry people are unhappy people. If there isn't food I'll sometimes bring it in because I think it's only fair to feed the people who are working hard for you. It doesn't hurt to buy a few cheese sandwiches.

I've heard some pretty shocking stories about peoples' riders. We always got wine gums in our dressing rooms backstage at *The X Factor*, but we never, ever got the black ones. A certain judge, who I won't name, only liked the black ones, so some poor runner used to have to go through packets and packets of them and sift them out. It was nice that we got free sweets, but my favourites are the black ones too, so I used to be gutted where there wasn't a single one to be found! I honestly can't think of anything worse than some poor sod having to do that for me. It's in my nature to make sure everyone else is all right before I am, so I would hate for anyone to feel like they have to bow down to me. In my opinion no one is better than anyone else in this world, regardless of job or background. I won't be demanding a bowl of yellow M&Ms anytime soon.

Sadly, when the smoking ban came in it kind of killed off clubs as we knew them. People wanted to be able to go to a club and sit down and have a drink and a fag, not have to go and stand outside in the cold every time they wanted to smoke. Because of that more and more people started to stay at home where they could do what they wanted in the comfort of their own living rooms. The social club numbers slowly dwindled and in 2002 I felt like the band was coming to its natural end; certainly for me it was. I missed my family and I wanted to move back down to London. I wanted to try my hand at acting and I found an agent who told me they were holding auditions for *EastEnders*. I was well up for it. I hadn't done any acting but I wasn't going to let that hold me back. I was mulling over how I was going to tell Tony and Gary and I was days away from breaking the news when, in (wait for it) another case of terrible timing, I met a guy and my plans kind of fell by the wayside.

Jason, as we'll call him, was a DJ in some of the clubs in Leicester. He was a good-looking lad and very sure of himself, always really well turned out in a nice shirt. One night when I was out with some mates we swapped numbers. I've always been quite insecure when it comes to men and whenever I've been out with people I've always thought 'What do they see in me?' I've never felt quite good enough for anyone. At the time I was slim with a six-pack and I dressed well, so I can't have looked too bad, but I didn't feel particularly attractive. Jason and I had a lot in common because we were both really into our music and we started hanging out together a lot. Before you can say 'turntable' we were a couple and all thoughts of London and *EastEnders* flew out of my head.

One night I was performing with the Tony Carnagie band in a club called Houston's in Leicester. Jason came along and he brought his mate Craig with him. One of my friends told me afterwards that when I walked out on stage Craig's jaw dropped because some of the outfits I wore didn't leave a lot – or indeed anything – to the imagination. I used to wear really tight dresses and bikinis and all sorts. A group of us went clubbing afterwards and when we went to get a taxi home I was freezing because I was wearing next to nothing. Jason was so busy chatting to his mates he hadn't even noticed I was almost blue and shivering, but Craig got his coat and wrapped it round me and I thought it was such a sweet thing to do.

I carried on seeing Jason and I did really like him, but I started to hear rumours that he was cheating on me. I went round to his house just after Valentine's Day and he had a slushy card from another girl up. He tried to tell me that one of his mates had sent it as a joke but I was nobody's fool. I put two and two together from all of the things I'd been hearing and it all made perfect sense, so I finished with him there and then. Shortly afterwards I started getting stomach aches and when I went to the doctor it turned out Jason had given me an STD. I was furious and it showed me that I'd definitely made the right decision. What an idiot. I couldn't believe someone else had cheated on me and I felt so let down, especially as I'd sacrificed opportunities for him. I decided I needed some time on my own and I threw myself back into work. I was still planning to go back to London but to go while I was still feeling hurt didn't feel right.

About a month later, on 2nd May 2002, I felt ready to go out and enjoy myself again, so one Friday night some mates and I went out clubbing in Leicester. They always say that you find love when you least expect it and I certainly wasn't looking for it that night. It was the last thing on my mind. I was still angry about the situation with Jason and I wasn't looking to get into another relationship. I just wanted to have a good time with my friends.

My mates and I were all on the dance floor when this weird guy came over and started dancing far too close to us for it to be comfortable. It all felt a bit pervy and wrong, so I left the dance floor to get a drink. The first person I bumped into was Craig and I immediately thought 'This night is not going well at all'. The last person I wanted to see was Jason, and the second-to-last people were Jason's mates. This was one of the very rare nights when I'd had a couple of drinks, so my guard was down a bit and Craig and I started chatting. After about an hour my flatmate Melissa shouted over, 'Are you two going to kiss or what?' With that, Craig leant over and snogged me! It was so weird because I'd always thought he was a nice guy, but I'd never thought of him in *that* way because I'd been with Jason. I would never look at another guy romantically if I was already attached; to me he was just 'Jason's nice mate'.

As soon as Craig and I started kissing I knew I liked him. The attraction between us was massive. I remember going to the loo and I got a text from him saying, 'Where are you babe?' He'd thought I'd done a runner and left him! At the end of the night we had a bit of a slow dance to Will Young's 'Evergreen' while we were waiting for our cabs to arrive and he was so lovely to me. I can't explain why but he felt different to other guys somehow. I felt happy just being around him, and I know it's a cliché but we got on so well it was like we'd known each other for years.

When we all piled into the taxis Melissa said to Craig, 'You can come back to our flat if you like?' I was really hoping he'd say no because I didn't want him to think he was going to get lucky, but in the end we sat up all night talking on the sofa. He left early the next morning and I felt genuinely sad when he went. I had a gig that night and on the way in the van something inside me clicked and I knew I had to text him. Forget being cool and playing games, I liked this guy and life's too short. I sent him a text asking if he wanted to go for dinner the following night and he sent me a message straight back saying, 'Sorry, I always go to my mum's for Sunday dinner.' I was wounded – he'd blown me out for his mum's cooking! I resigned myself to the fact he wasn't interested because I hadn't slept with him so I replied with a really causal text saying, 'No problem. Let's leave it'. Later that night I got a phone call from him saying that he'd cancelled Sunday dinner because he really wanted to see me. Yeeeeeees!

For our very first date we went to the Toby Carvery in Leicester. Afterwards he wanted to show me where he lived and he drove me to the house we still live in now. Back then everything was blue and it was a proper lads' pad. His wardrobe had about five shirts in it and his kitchen cupboards were pretty much empty. He was a full-on bachelor. I started going round every day to hang out and then he'd drop me back at home in the evening. After about two weeks he said nervously, 'Why don't you stay the night?' and from then on we became a proper couple.

I went from coming over during the day to staying the night to never going home. Within two weeks my toothbrush was in the bathroom and within about a month I'd moved in permanently. Obviously I immediately started making the place more girlie and homely so it felt more like *our* place. I also made him get rid of any traces of ex-girlfriends. Anything that had a link to an ex went into the bin. Even though Craig made me really happy, the old insecurities were still hanging around.

I know for a fact I wasn't easy when I first got together with Craig because I was convinced he was going to cheat on me like the other guys. If he was in a pub and I called and heard a girl's voice in the background I would threaten to leave him because I'd convince myself that he was being unfaithful. I must have been a nightmare. He couldn't go anywhere or do anything because I was sure that he either had already cheated on me or he was going to. It was a difficult time because I needed reassurance, but I also didn't want him to feel stifled or push him away. Craig handled it brilliantly and responded by being deeply romantic and making me feel so secure. It was the first time someone had properly taken care of me rather than me taking on the mothering role.

I got back from a gig once and Craig told me that I had to go straight upstairs and have a bath and I wasn't allowed to look out of the windows. When I came back downstairs he'd made a picnic in the garden and lit candles. It was the loveliest thing a boyfriend had ever done for me. He used to leave teddies out with notes saying 'I'm your teddy' and he'd plan nights out for us. He'll kill me for telling you all of this because his mates will give him hell!

Before long we were making a proper commitment to each other. We got a dog. She was a springer spaniel called Molly and we've still got her to this day. She's a bit old and smelly now but she's still lovely. She's been with us through everything and I don't know what I'll do if anything happens to her. She's such a big part of our family and our kids love her.

I continued singing with the band and in January 2003 Danny Davies called me and asked if I would be interested in entering the Eurovision Song Contest because he had a song he wanted to submit. I had my reservations because it's a bit of a car crash and the UK always ends up with nil points. Some of the events I would have to commit to also clashed with our upcoming holiday in Thailand, which Craig was really loathe to cut short. He was so insistent that we had to go on this holiday and enjoy it in its entirety and I had no idea why. I assumed he was worried about my ego getting bruised if I was a Euro-flop. But I soon out found the real reason.

I let Danny down gently and put the Eurovision opportunity to the back of my mind. In February Craig and I jetted off to Thailand for this amazing two-week holiday. One night we were in Bangkok and neither of us could sleep. We'd both taken presents for each other for Valentine's Day, so we got them out of the safe and I sat on the bed waiting for him to come and open his. All of sudden he fell to his knees and I thought he'd fallen over. Then suddenly he burst out, 'Will you marry me?' I think we all know what my answer was… I was completely overwhelmed. I honestly wasn't expecting it but it was the best surprise in the world. We had another ten days in Pattaya to look forward to and we spent the whole time celebrating. When we got home we had a big engagement party at Tony and Gary's and I don't think I stopped smiling all night.

Craig and I sat down and talked about what we wanted do for our big day. I think because my parents were no longer together I didn't want a big traditional do. We weighed up the options and decided to get married in Las Vegas. We remortgaged the house and took out £25,000 so we had money to do the things we most wanted. We had a conservatory built on to the house, new windows and also booked Vegas. We decided to have the ceremony with just the two of us but to have an Internet wedding so our friends and family could watch a live feed of the ceremony back home in their pyjamas with a bottle of wine. They could even sign the wedding book online. It seemed like a great solution.

In January 2004 we were all ready to go. My mum had bought me a wedding dress and I chose something very simple. We were planning to go out straight after the wedding and I would have looked ridiculous walking around Vegas in a big meringue. We stayed in a hotel in Manchester the night before our flight and the following morning we boarded the plane. We were all ready to take off and I was feeling so nervous because I'm not a good flyer. Then suddenly one of the other passengers said there was smoke coming out of the plane. The next thing I knew we were all herded off and told the flight had been cancelled. Brilliant. We were *so* gutted. The airline told us we could either wait for the next direct flight or transfer to one that changed in Washington.

We were desperate to get out there so we decided to go for the first available flight. We told the staff we were heading out to get married and, amazingly, we got upgraded to business class. It was so lavish and they kept bringing us over champagne and nibbles. Every time they gave me a glass of bubbly I'd wait for them to turn their backs and then give it to Craig. By the time we got to Washington to change flights I was stuffed full of food and Craig was absolutely steaming! We finally arrived in Vegas tired but happy (and, in Craig's case, still pretty drunk) at about one in the morning, and waited at the carousel for our luggage. And we waited. *No* luggage. I just knew instinctively that it had gone on another flight. My wedding dress and my shoes were in my suitcase and all I had were the clothes I was standing up in and my handbag. It was the same for Craig (minus the handbag!). We spoke to an airport official who told us in an annoyingly calm voice that they'd send our luggage on to our hotel as soon as it arrived, but I was livid.

We jumped into a taxi to our hotel, the MGM Grand, and went to check in straight away. We were beyond tired by then. Craig gave our names and after a couple of minutes the receptionist gave us a confused look and said, 'Sorry, we've got no record of your booking.' I had a printout of the booking confirmation with me but for some reason we weren't registered. The receptionist headed off to try and sort something out I turned to Craig and said only half-joking, 'Something's telling us we shouldn't be getting married!'

Eventually the receptionist came back and told us he'd been able to upgrade us to a suite. Result! We had two bedrooms, two bathrooms and a living area – it was huge. So while everything may have been going wrong up until that point, at least we were being upgraded every step of the way. But there was still no sign of our luggage. I was pacing up and down the room because we couldn't get to sleep. We didn't even have a toothbrush or deodorant, let alone anything to change into. We weren't due to get married until three days later, so at least we had a bit of time to try and get our suitcases back, but needless to say I was panicking. At about 4am we went downstairs because we were still wide awake, and noticed there was a big McDonald's in the lobby – and it was just opening. That was the best thing that could have happened to me in that moment. I needed a big McDonald's hug. We must have looked like a pair of tramps sat in there just as the sun was coming up eating McMuffins.

About an hour later our luggage arrived and I've never felt so relieved. Craig hired a tux in Vegas and the morning of the wedding I went to the New York New York hotel to get my hair done. So many people get married in Vegas that no one batted an eyelid when we walked through the lobby in our wedding attire.

At 3.30pm on 29th January, Craig and I tied the knot in front of our (virtual!) loved ones. We both giggled all the way through our vows. Craig couldn't get his words out and that made me laugh even more. We were waving to people at home via the webcam and it was all very light-hearted and fun, which is exactly how we both wanted it to be.

After the wedding we got taken by limousine to a helipad and then went on an incredible helicopter ride over the Hoover Dam. We had booked a nice restaurant for dinner, so afterwards we got a boat across Lake Mead – past all of these amazing houses that are owned by the likes of Celine Dion and Nicolas Cage – to this amazing five-star restaurant. It was a beautiful place but I think I *may* have mentioned before how fussy I am with food. I ordered the beef wellington but when it arrived it was so rare it was practically still mooing and there was no way I could have eaten it. We were in this amazing place and yet all I was doing was dreaming of McDonald's back in the hotel. Our waiter was so lovely I called him over and said as quietly as possible, 'I could kill for some egg and chips. Is there any chance I can get some?' He said he'd speak to the head chef, and several minutes later this big, angry-looking Scottish guy came walking out of the kitchen towards us. He started taking the mickey out of me about my meal request and I replied, 'I'm not being funny but I've just got married and I'm not very good with fancy food.' He smiled and nodded and then went back into the kitchen and sent out the fanciest egg and chips I've ever seen. He'd even made a turret out of the chips! It was one of the best meals I've ever had.

Craig filmed the entire boat journey back, proudly doing his tourist bit and explaining what was what and who lived where. Unfortunately he'd forgotten to take the lens cap off the video camera so all we've got on that section of our wedding video is Craig's voice and a whole lot of black.

When we got back to the hotel Craig tried to be all romantic and carry me over the threshold, but he ended up banging my head on the doorframe. Oh dear. I changed into my Leicester City tracksuit and Craig put on shorts and a top and we finished the night off at McDonald's. While everything may not have been perfect, our wedding was definitely memorable.

We had a couple more days in Vegas as a married couple

and had a wicked time. We went to see Celine Dion at Caesars Palace and Craig bought me a signed photo as a present that we hung in our conservatory as soon as we got home. Next we flew on to Florida. Craig had never been before and he was like a little kid. He was running everywhere and he was so excited. We went to the theme parks, the perfect ending to our wedding.

When we got back to Leicester we hired out Braunstone Social Club and had a big party for all of our friends and family. We had a disco with karaoke and hired a bucking bronco. I got a special trophy for the winner and we piled tables high with food. Craig and I had our first dance to 'So Amazing' by Luther Vandross, and instead of a big wedding cake we had six tiers of French Fancies, because they're my absolute favourites. My mum and dad both came and even though they spent the entire night at different ends of the room it was great to have them there. My dad, bless him, kept trying to get my mum to dance with him because he still loved her to pieces but she wasn't even the tiniest bit interested.

CHAPTER 7

HELLO, GOODBYE

Shortly before we'd got married I started learning to drive. Craig and I were planning our future and we knew that if we had kids I needed to be able to get out and about on my own when he was at work. So after lots and lots of lessons, in August 2004, I took my test and passed it first time. Craig had bought me a little Fiesta that I called Ronnie after my dad, and I went straight to Asda to do a shop because I was so excited that I could zoom around on my own. I loved driving and I used to make excuses to go out just so I could take the car. Craig took me out on the motorway a couple of times so I could get used to it and then a couple of weeks later I drove all the way to my mum's in Kent. I was bursting with pride when I arrived.

It was just as well I *had* learned to drive because in 2005 we found out that we were about to have another addition to our family. Yes, I was pregnant. Because I had really irregular periods due to cysts on my ovaries I never really knew when I was due to have one. Craig and I had decided we were going to try for a baby and within two weeks I was pregnant. I remember my boobs were tingling so I did suspect, and when a test confirmed it we went totally crazy. It was the best news ever.

I couldn't have been happier but I was still in the band, so I had to break the news to Tony that I would be leaving. He was really happy for me but obviously it meant that he had to find a replacement, which was a bit of a headache. I carried on doing the shows for as long as I could, and I was wearing bigger and bigger clothes as the weeks went by. The Tony Carnagie show got booked to do a gig in Dubai and Craig came along with me; it was when we were lying in our hotel room that Craig felt the baby kick for the first time.

Those kinds of gigs were rare but amazing. Toyota was launching a new car and we were the entertainment, so we got so do the show at the Jumeirah Beach Hotel. I was in maternity clothes but the rest of the band couldn't wear half of their outfits because they were a bit racy for Dubai, so poor Tony had to spend a fortune buying things that were a bit more conservative.

I had a relatively good pregnancy. I didn't have any morning sickness or anything and the only thing I experienced were a few strange mood swings. I burst into tears when we were playing a game of cards with some friends in our living room once because I thought Craig was trying to cheat. I knew I was being irrational but I ran upstairs and cried so much I thought I was going to throw up. It was so weird. Thankfully I wasn't like that all of the time, but there was the odd occasion when I felt completely out of control. That's hormones for you, I guess.

We decided to find out the sex of the baby and I was petrified when I first found out I was having a girl. Having grown up with two brothers and been a tomboy all my life I wasn't sure how I would cope. I wouldn't know how to do her hair or what to dress her in. I didn't play with dollies when I was growing up; I was too busy playing with mud or a football, so how would I know what she would and wouldn't like? It was definitely going to be a steep learning curve.

When I was 32 weeks gone, the band went to do a gig at New Lodge Working Men's Club in Barnsley. Craig came with us to do the lighting and we had to stop at every single service station so I could go to the toilet. I didn't think anything of it because you always wee a lot more when you're pregnant, but as soon as I went I wanted to go again.

We went on stage and started the show and every time I sang a powerful note I thought I was going to wet myself. When we did the last number, a medley of rock songs, I thought I was going to have to leave the stage to run to the toilet. I'd never been pregnant before but I still had eight weeks to go and knew something wasn't right. My trousers were soaked but Craig reassured me that everything was fine and we put it down to pregnancy bladder weakness.

We drove back to Leicester, stopping wherever possible, and when we arrived home I called the Leicester Royal Infirmary hospital. They told me to head straight up there to get checked out. I had an internal and they broke the news to me that my waters had broken. It was crazy because I hadn't experienced any contractions or anything and apart from the constant weeing I didn't really have any other symptoms. My pregnancy had been so straightforward and all I'd experienced was some lower back pain. The doctor was telling me all of the things that could be wrong with the baby and I was like a terrified deer trapped in headlights because it all sounded so negative.

We had everything ready back home for our baby. Her bedroom was all kitted out, the pushchair had been ordered and we had loads of little clothes ready for her to wear. And here we were being told that something could go wrong with my pregnancy.

I had to stay in hospital so the doctors could monitor me. They were worried that the baby might be premature, which meant that her organs might not be fully developed. I was given a series of injections to speed up the growth process and a few days later a doctor told me that they were going to induce my labour and I was going to have the baby that day.

The hospital phoned Craig to tell him to come as soon as he could, but he's a service engineer and he was out on a job in Northampton at the time. He had one of those stickers on the back of his van that says 'how am I driving' and you can imagine the number of complaints his office got when he was tearing down the hard shoulder at 70mph to get to me.

I was all over the place, lying in the bed thinking 'What if this baby isn't ready to come out yet? What if she's not okay?' Then all of a sudden the doctor said that her heart rate was dropping and I would have to have a C-section. Gary was by my side constantly and said he was going to come into the delivery room with me while I gave birth if Craig couldn't get there in time. He was like a mum, holding my hand and saying soothing words to me.

Thankfully Craig got there just before I was wheeled into theatre. He was gowned up, and after I'd been given a rather painful steroid injection, it was time. I had a screen covering half of me so I couldn't see what was going on, but when I felt a tickle I knew they were cutting me. Next I felt a hand go inside me, and about 20 minutes later I heard a small cry. They held my little baby Brooke over the screen for me to see and she was *so* tiny, 4lb 14oz and like a little dot. I was stitched up and taken to a recovery area where I fell straight to sleep. When I woke up Craig told me Brooke had been taken to Leicester General Hospital by ambulance because she wasn't feeding properly. I hadn't even had a chance to hold her. I was told I could go and see her either that evening or the following day, but I needed to be with my child immediately.

I got myself dressed and we drove to the General. I was being sick into a cardboard hospital tray for the entire journey and when I arrived the staff were furious that I'd travelled without a doctor or a nurse after such major surgery. The staff at the General were amazing and my mum travelled straight up to see me. Because Brooke was so small none of the clothes we had bought fitted her, so she was wearing a hospital babygrow and this little blue knitted hat that had been donated by the local Women's Institute. The hospital was right next to Mothercare, so Craig had to go and buy a load of early-baby clothes for her. When he brought them back they were like dolls clothes they were so small. It was hard to imagine that my baby could be so little.

My milk hadn't started to come through, so Brooke was being fed thought a tube and that mortified me. I felt like I'd failed her. I was trying everything but after two days the head midwife wheeled me down to see Brooke and told me take off her sleep suit. She explained that the hormone that's usually released when you give birth to a baby hadn't been because I'd had the caesarean. She told me to sniff the sleep suit and they took a Polaroid picture of Brooke for me to look at to try and stimulate the hormone. I thought she was playing a joke on me. I honestly thought there were cameras in the room and it was all a bit of a laugh. How on earth was that going to work? But I was willing to try anything.

The midwife left the room and I sat there looking at the photo and sniffing the sleep suit, feeling utterly ridiculous. I'm not joking, within an hour I could physically see my boobs getting bigger and filling up with milk. Within about three hours I looked like Jordan. I phoned Craig laughing my head off and said, 'Oh my god, my boobs are massive! They're like pillows!'

As soon as my milk came in I felt so much better but Brooke still wouldn't latch on. I was allowed to go home after a week but Brooke had to stay in and be monitored, which I was gutted about. I was told that I had to express milk for her so I was sat in front of the TV with these two breast pumps crying my eyes out because I wanted to be with my baby. I desperately wanted her at home with us so we could start being a proper family.

I went and visited her every day to take milk in and be with her. Craig used to sit in the armchair next to the tiny bed with Brooke on his chest for hours. After she'd been in there for about five days I got a phone call asking if I wanted to 'room in' with Brooke that night. Rooming in is where you share a bedroom with your baby and all being well take them home the following day. The night went brilliantly, so at long last Craig and I got to bring our baby home. She was still so small but she was really good and barely cried. We set up a camera and a monitor in her bedroom but I still couldn't relax. I guess all new mums must be a bit like that. I used to sit staring at her Moses basket all night making sure she was okay. I hardly slept but I had to make sure she was safe and had everything she needed.

I loved being a mum and I didn't mind doing the night feeds; I just napped as and when I could. Craig was brilliant and he helped me with the cooking and cleaning and looked after Brooke when he wasn't working. Things were still a bit of a struggle for me because I still had stitches and I was walking a bit like John Wayne for a while. I must admit the tiredness did get to me a bit sometimes. But it was well worth it. She was so beautiful.

Not surprisingly after everything we'd been through, I didn't feel much like going out for a little while. But when Brooke was a couple of months old Craig and I got invited to a party at our local rugby club. My mum and my brother Danny came to stay to look after Brooke and I decided to brave my first social event since I'd had her.

Craig was in the garden just before we were due to leave and he heard a massive crash and then the sound of a car horn. We both ran through the alley near our house and we were faced with the most horrific scene. Two cars had crashed into each other and this elderly couple were involved. I saw this old lady lying on the pavement and I went over and started talking to her. I knew that she needed to stay conscious, so I was asking her where her pain was and if she was on any medication or had any allergies. I was telling her all about Brooke and I assured her that her husband was okay. I didn't even think about it; it was just instinctive.

I know that pain makes you go into shock and once that happens it can be fatal. We covered her in coats and when the police and ambulance arrived I said, 'This is Beryl, she's 72. She's complaining about pain in her left hip. She's allergic to so and so and she's not taking this medication.' The medic looked at me really seriously and said, 'Are you a doctor?' and I replied, 'No, I just watch *Holby City* mate!'

Beryl was taken off in an ambulance and when Craig and I walked back to the house I felt like I'd been in some kind of dream world. I didn't know I was capable of doing something like that. I bumped into a friend a few days later and he said, 'You know you're in the *Leicester Mercury* don't you?' The *Leicester Mercury* is our local paper and Beryl had written a letter thanking me for helping her and wishing me good luck with Brooke. She also sent a letter to me with a cheque for £25, so I cashed it and went straight to the florists and sent her a bunch of flowers. I didn't help her for any other reason than because I could and I certainly didn't want any kind of reward. It turned out that she'd broken her hip, but thankfully she did make a full recovery afterwards.

I didn't do any gigs for a long time after having Brooke because I wanted to stay at home with her. I'd started a childcare course while I was pregnant, so I carried on with that and settled into life as a mum. Brooke had quite bad reflux issues – I'd feed her and then two minutes later she would projectile vomit across the room. I was on the phone to NHS Direct a *lot* and we had ambulances coming to the house quite frequently. When she was about eight months old she had to go back into hospital because she had a really high temperature. It was a very scary time, but it turned out she had a virus and she was fine again within a few days. I think because she was my first child and she'd been premature I was so much more aware of every tiny little scratch or rash. But she grew up to be a strong little girl and she's hardly ever ill now.

Craig started working with Gary and Tony on the road quite a lot, helping out at the gigs. He used to pretend to play keyboards on stage but he was actually controlling the lights. People used to compliment him on his piano skills but he didn't even know to play! It was like the tables had turned and instead of me being on stage in front of a room full of people, it was him. Not that I was in the right place to be getting up on stage at that time. I put on a lot of weight with Brooke and had severe water retention. It was the first time I'd ever had cankles. My calves and feet were as one; you couldn't see my ankles at all. I wasn't rushing to get back to my pre-baby weight but I became very aware that I was bigger. I remember Craig doing some filming of Brooke and I, and when I bent over he genuinely had to zoom out with the camera to get Brooke and my backside in the same shot. I was so upset when I saw it that I deleted the footage. I used to make jokes about my seven chins and bingo wings but I really wasn't happy.

In my eyes I looked huge. I'd been a size 8–10 before I got pregnant and I really did balloon. I asked Craig to buy me a gym membership for my birthday so I could get back into shape but I was too tired to go. I was still doing loads of night feeds, so during the day I'd be like a zombie and not really in the mood to get on a treadmill or lift weights. My weight eventually went down naturally but it took months and months. Even when I did lose the pounds (well, stones) I didn't go back to a size eight. I kind of resigned myself to the fact that those days were over and I was fine with being a slim size ten.

Tony always said I was welcome back in the band but I didn't rejoin them until a good six months after I'd had Brooke. I didn't feel ready before then. Of course the outfits that I'd worn pre-pregnancy were no longer suitable for me. There was no way I was going to parade around in a red sequined bikini again! We had to go out and buy some new outfits, so I was wearing smart suits and dresses and I soon started to feel more like my old self. We changed the show a lot and it was like we entered a new phase, which reignited my interest.

I did need to be working and bringing money in but it was hard when the band had to go away for long periods of time. I did a week of Christmas parties up in Scotland that December and when I came home Brooke almost looked right through me. She wasn't excited to see me at all. She was about eight months old but she barely batted an eyelid and instead crawled over to Craig. I vowed then that I would never go away for that long again. I loved singing but it was more important for me to stay at home. I cut right back on the gigs and if I really needed to get a singing fix I'd go to one of my local pubs and do some karaoke so I could get it out of my system.

In 2007 my life changed forever when my dad became very ill. He was always petrified of the dentist, much like I am, so when he thought he had an abscess in his mouth he didn't do anything about it for some time. When he eventually did go to the dentist he was told he needed to go to hospital and have it looked at as soon as possible. It turned out to be mouth cancer, which was a devastating diagnosis, and he was started on a course of radiotherapy. He had a big lump in his neck and his mouth and the next time I saw him he looked like a different man. It was so sad to see him like that and all I could do was pray that the treatment would work.

I'll never forget getting the phone call from my nan in the spring of 2007 telling me that my dad's cancer was terminal. I was devastated. They didn't give us any idea of time but I couldn't imagine him not being here. He'd always been such a huge part of my life and I think I almost went into shock and tried to stop myself thinking about the inevitable. My nan kept me up to date with how he was in between; she went round to his house every day to deliver him beer, which may not have been the most sensible thing for him to have, but it was like his medicine and it was how he got through each day.

I'd applied for *The X Factor* a few months before, and I

had my audition a few days after I found out about dad. I didn't want to go along and use my dad's illness as an excuse in case people thought it was some sob story, so I didn't tell any of the researchers what was going on. I went along to Birmingham NEC wearing a ladies' Leicester City tracksuit and after singing 'His Eye Is On The Sparrow' by Lauryn Hill for about a minute I was given a firm 'no'. They told me to keep practising and come back the following year. I was so deflated when I walked out of there, I vowed there and then that I would never do it again. I was totally myself and I sang my little heart out and it wasn't enough. I honestly wondered if I'd have fared better if I'd mentioned that my dad was unwell. I was so sceptical that in my head I believed you were only successful if you had a sob story, but I wasn't about to try and use a horribly sad situation to try and get ahead. As far as I was concerned *The X Factor* and I were done.

In January 2008 my nan called me to tell me my dad had passed away. She'd gone round to see him and found him in bed, looking like he was fast asleep. When my nan told me about my dad I remember falling to the floor and shouting, 'No, no, no, no.' My neighbour Yvonne came running in and she called Craig at work to let him know. I was supposed to be doing a gig that night but I had to cancel – there was no way I could get up on stage.

I was in bits. Yvonne offered to look after Brooke for us, so Craig took some time off work and we drove straight to my mum's house. By the time we got there Dad's body had been taken to a funeral parlour, which was a few doors up from Mum's house. They had already closed by the time I got there but I walked up to the window and pressed my nose up against it. I could see a door at the back of the room and I knew his body was being stored behind it. I remember counting how many metres away from me he would have been in that moment and it broke my heart.

My nan went round to start sorting out his belongings, and she found more than 300 full cans of Special Brew hidden away in various places. He obviously hadn't been drinking all the beer she'd been taking him, after all. She also found a note he'd written saying 'I want a 'kin wake', meaning he wanted 'a fucking wake'. He also said he wanted his guitars shared out between his sister Jackie and I, and he also wanted a brass band playing 'When the Saints Go Marching In' so it would be an uplifting day, not a sad one.

I still feel guilty now that I didn't see him more when he was ill. I didn't realise how sick he was. My nan told me that the hospital had upped his morphine in his final few weeks, but no one told me about it. Had I known I would have suspected he didn't have much longer left and would have taken time off work to go and be with him. I've still got dad's journals up in my loft. He was writing down his thoughts and ideas but I can't bring myself to read them. Maybe one day I will, but right now it still feels too raw.

Going back to dad's house for the first time was so strange.

My nan was there, but it still felt empty somehow. I went up to Dad's room and saw that my nan had picked out a suit for him to wear for the funeral. My dad *hated* wearing suits. It was hanging over the back of the chair and all of a sudden it fell to the floor. I just thought, 'I've got to do something here', so I went downstairs with dad's favourite grey collarless silk shirt and said to my nan that I thought he should wear that instead. I was waiting for her to go mad at me because she was very fierce, but surprisingly she backed down. I took the shirt into the funeral parlour later that day, along with a smart pair of trousers. I also took along photos of my mum and dad, some of me, Danny and Charlie and some of the grandkids. I asked the funeral director to put them in his pocket on the day of the funeral. If my nan had found that picture of Mum and Dad together she would have gone crazy because Mum and her didn't get on at all; they'd had a massive fallout years before. There was a lot of slapping involved and they hadn't spoken since.

Dad's funeral didn't take place until three weeks after he died and those three weeks were some of the worst of my life. I hated the fact my dad, who I'd worshipped, was in a bloody fridge. The day before the funeral I went round to my nan's to help sort everything out for the wake and she told me that she'd given Jenny, the woman my dad had *that* affair with, one of dad's guitars. It was the only one I wanted and I was so angry. Dad had been given that guitar after his best friend, who I called Uncle Mickey, was killed in a car crash. I knew how much it meant to him and I knew he would want it to stay in the family. My nan was like the don of our family. She was in charge of everyone and everything and you didn't mess with her. I was so furious my blood was boiling, but I didn't have the energy to say anything to her because I knew it would lead to a row. To be fair to Jenny, she was the one who really helped look after my dad when he was ill, but I was still really upset that the one thing I really wanted – and my dad wanted me to have – had been given to her.

Later that day, my nan said she was going to see my dad in the funeral parlour and asked if I wanted to go along. I was in two minds about whether or not I wanted to see him, so she told me what time she would be there and said, 'If you're there, you're there. If you're not, we understand.' I went back to my mum's house and to take my mind off things I started playing darts on her board. I said to myself, 'If I get a 20, I'm going to see my dad. If I don't, I won't.' I was aiming for 20 and I was so desperate to get it that I'd already answered my own question really. I knew I wanted to go. Something told me I needed to.

I got to the funeral parlour a bit early and when I saw Dad my first thought was 'he looks like marble'. The lump was gone from his neck, his hair was washed, his face had been shaved and he looked really smart. I put my fingers through his hair and it felt so soft. I was stroking his head and I was so glad I'd gone to see him. I would have really regretted it if I hadn't.

The funeral itself was incredibly emotional. I wore a

bright yellow T-shirt with the band Budgie on it. Dad would have loved it. They played Phil Collins' 'In the Air Tonight' and when the drum solo kicked in I burst into tears because it reminded me so much of Dad. In my head I could see him playing along. I was sat right at the front and when I turned around all of Dad's musician friends were playing air drums as a mark of respect. There were flowers in the shape of drums and Gibson Les Paul guitars, and at the wake people were telling me all of these stories about what my dad had got up to in the good old days. I was pretty shocked about some of them! All of the rock'n'roll stuff came out and it seemed my dad had lived quite a life.

The night I arrived back in Leicester I was bathing Brooke and she kept looking up to the ceiling and waving. I asked her who she was waving at and she said, 'Pop', which is what she called my dad. I can only assume that one of my neighbours must have told her about my dad dying, but it was quite comforting in a way.

The only things I kept of my dad's are some pyjamas, a Supertramp T-shirt from when I took him to their concert, a clock and a cup and saucer. I didn't want or need much stuff, but his guitar kept playing on my mind. A few months after the funeral I called Jenny and told her that Dad had wanted me to have it. She was really apologetic and said, 'Come and get it whenever you want. It's yours.' She was so understanding about it. We've become good friends over the years. Who could have predicted that?

The only other thing I wanted were some of Dad's ashes, but when I asked my nan for them she told me she'd already sprinkled them all in his garden. I was really hurt, so I took it upon myself to go to his house and ask the new owners if I could have some soil from their garden. I knew it sounded a bit crazy and the new owners were understandably very taken aback. But bless them, they let me do it.

I called my nan afterwards to tell her what I'd done and she must have felt bad because she said, 'Sam, come round. I've got some of the ashes here.' When I arrived she had a carnelian, which is my dad's favourite plant, and she'd mixed the ashes in with the soil, so she gave me some to take home.

I planted a carnelian in my back garden and sprinkled the ashes around it. Every night when I used to go outside for my last cigarette I would look up at the sky. My dad loved astrology and he always used to show us things like Orion's Belt and Pegasus. I was always looking for a sign from him, like a shooting star, so I'd spend ages looking up and hoping. I also used to look in my wing mirror when I was driving in the hope of seeing him sitting on the back seat smiling at me. I wanted to know he was still around. I was desperate for something. *Anything.* I missed him so much.

CHAPTER 8

JAILHOUSE ROCK

I decided I wanted to go out singing on my own so I went to a 'shop window', which is a showcase in a social club where singers who want to get booked on the circuit can go along and sing for venue owners. I met up with a girl called Erin, an agent, who I'd spoken to briefly on the phone a few times. We were outside having a cigarette and she turned to me and said, 'I only know two Sams. You're one and the other one is a relative of mine. I went to see a psychic a while ago and she said to me, "You'll work with someone called Sam", and she said that I had to say three things to you. It may sound crazy but I have to say them because it's driving me insane.'

I thought it was a bit odd because we didn't even know each other, and I wasn't sure I believed in all of that anyway. Then she paused and said to me, 'Walt Disney World Florida, the Twin Towers and Sex With Strangers.' As I've mentioned I was in Disney World when the planes hit the Twin Towers, and of course Sex With Strangers was the band my dad was in when I was young.

I felt physically sick. There's no way she could have known any of those things about me. It played on my mind so much, but I took it as being the sign I needed.

A while later I was talking to my cousin Clare on Facebook about a psychic she'd been to see and the woman had described me and said, 'Tell that lady that's out in the garden looking up at the sky hoping to see a shooting star that he's right beside her.' I'd never told anyone that I did that. It was my little secret and it totally freaked me out.

I had a similar experience about two years ago when we went to my husband's auntie's house to see a medium. There were about ten of us and one woman came through who was stern, and I thought it was my dad's mum because she was very authoritarian. The message she channelled was for me to stop looking in the wing mirror. She also said she saw a piece of paper with 'Chasing Cars' written on it in red pen. The second part didn't resonate with me at all, but I was doing a gig a short time later and I opened up my tracks case. Inside was a piece of paper with 'Chasing Cars' written on it in red pen. Someone had put in a request for me to sing it at a previous gig but I'd completely forgotten about it. I've still got that piece of paper to this day.

Shortly after my dad died his sister, Jackie, also passed

away. She was so like my dad. They both had guitars, they both liked a drink and they were so close. I went to London for her funeral and the night before I was sleeping on my mum's sofa. I was drifting off to sleep and the entire room went cold and I had this feeling that someone was standing behind me. The thought came into my head that it was my dad and Auntie Jackie standing there hand in hand, and then the room went warm again. I like to think it was my dad letting me know that he's okay. It was the most bizarre thing I've ever experienced in my life and I get emotional just thinking about it. I know a lot of people are sceptical but I genuinely can't explain away any of those things.

My dad was always in my thoughts and I'm so gutted that Tommy, my son, will never meet him and Brooke probably won't remember him. I've got an old phone that I can never get rid of because it's got photos and videos of my dad reading to Brooke on it that are so precious to me. I'll never stop missing him.

I lost both of my granddads and my nan shortly after my Auntie Jackie passed away. Pop, my dad's dad, passed away from emphysema. I remember someone saying to me, 'When you hit a certain age you'll need a black tie because you go to so many funerals.' And sadly they weren't wrong.

I carried on performing with The Tony Carnagie band for the next couple of years on and off, while also branching out on my own. I was still enjoying being in the show but the cracks were starting to show. I'd been in the band for years and I'd really worked my way up. Then a new girl called Gina joined the group and I found out that she was being paid more money than me and Tony was also reimbursing her for her petrol. I felt so disappointed that I'd worked so hard for so long and yet she was getting better treatment than I was. If I had a gig on a Friday evening I'd have to put Brooke into a nursery for the afternoon until Craig could collect her and I never once asked for that to be paid for. That incident was the straw that broke the camel's back and I knew I had to leave the band once and for all. I didn't want to stay and feel resentful towards someone I cared about so much, but first I needed to have a back-up plan.

Sadly, because of the recession and the smoking ban the gigs had started to dry up even more anyway. I'd get a call from Tony the night before a booking saying, 'Sorry, the gig tomorrow night's been cancelled because the club closed down last week.' I'd have been counting on that money, so I'd be left praying that someone else would book us for that slot so I could pay my phone bill.

The problem was other bands were willing to work for much less money than us, so we would often get undercut and miss out on performances. A lot of clubs seemed to stop caring whether or not the acts were actually any *good*; it was just about getting punters though the door and hoping they were too drunk to care if the band were crap. Sheffield and Rotherham used to be two of our biggest markets because there was a social club on every corner, but the majority of places now have solo performers because that's all they can afford. As a result, the solo market is really competitive, and that started to affect our bookings. People were willing to work for next to nothing and sometimes what we was offered for a performance would barely even cover our petrol.

I was worried about how long I could last doing singing off my own bat if I did leave the band, so I started to think long and hard about what else I could do with my life. Weirdly it was doing my weekly shop that kick-started my new career! A neighbour of mine was a prison officer and he'd told me lots of stories about his job which I found fascinating. One day when I walked into Asda, the prison service had set up a recruitment table near the entrance. I took an application form home, filled it in and sent it off. I had to do an online grammar and maths test, which I passed, and I received a letter inviting me to a Recruitment Assessment Day at Birmingham Prison. I had to take two more tests and then I was put into a room with actors and I had to explain how I would deal with certain situations and what the appropriate action would be. It was all filmed and my body language analysed to see how empathetic I was. I also had to have an interview. Thankfully I passed everything with flying colours.

The next step was a fitness test at Prison Service training college. I was incredibly nervous because the further along the process I got, the more I wanted the job. It was August 2008 and as I was getting ready to leave the house and head to the college I started to feel a bit unwell. My boobs were sore and I was feeling really tired, but I put it out of my mind and took the test. I passed no problem, which meant I'd completed all stages and I was in line to become a prison officer. It was brilliant news.

I drove home on a real high, but you don't automatically get a job when you pass all of the tests: you're put on a waiting list for three different prisons and when jobs come up the service contacts you to let you know. All I could do was hope a vacancy came up near me. Even once it did I'd have to spend six weeks at training college before I could actually start a job, so I kept my fingers crossed that something would come up sooner rather than later.

I was on cloud nine thinking I could be about to start a whole new career within weeks or months, but when I got home I still didn't feel right. And I was pretty sure I knew what it was. I went and bought a pregnancy test and – you guessed it – it turned out to be positive. There's that great Sam timing again! I phoned Craig and told him I'd passed the prison service fitness test and he was so pleased for me. Then I added, 'The only thing is, I've passed another test too. A pregnancy one!' I think it's fair to say he was *very* shocked but *very* happy.

I had no choice but to phone the prison service and tell them there was a *slight* problem with me carrying on with my application at that point. Training at Prison Service College would have involved me learning control and restraint and rolling about on the floor, and there's no way I could have done all of that pregnant. The lady I spoke to told me I had 18 months from the day I did my Recruitment Assessment Day to get back in touch and restart the process, so I marked it in my diary and carried on performing with Tony and the band.

It was getting harder and harder for us to keep going, and in 2009 we decided once and for all to go our separate ways. I think the spark had also gone from the show and Tony was getting sick of wearing leotards and prancing around a stage. He was constantly worrying about putting on weight and fitting into his outfits, and you can't really have a curvy Cher. I was also a mum and that kind of transient lifestyle really doesn't fit in very well with having children.

I'm still friends with Tony now, but we drifted apart a bit when the band broke up. He's living in Chesterfield and we'll always be mates, but what happened with Gina did make things difficult for a while, sadly. I have a lot of amazing memories from the years I spent performing with them though, and I also met one of my best mates, Jo, through the group, so I'll always be grateful. She's Brooke's godmother and she's absolutely blinding. The band was a massive part of my life and I was sad when it came to an end, but it had to at some point. I'll always feel proud of being a part of it because we made a lot of people happy over the years.

I knew I wanted to carry on singing in some way, so I decided to carry on doing some solo gigs as and when they came up. Craig bought me a little PA system, which meant

I could perform pretty much anywhere, and either Craig would come with me or I'd get someone at the venue to help me lift it onto the stage and get it up and running. It felt strange being on my own full-time after being surrounded by other performers for so long, but I had done enough solo gigs to feel confident about it and I soon got used to it. After my dad passed away my performances became more emotional and sometimes I would imagine he was sat at the back of the room nodding at me while I sang. That always kept me focused.

I went to sing at New Lodge Working Men's Club in Barnsley when I was about six or seven weeks pregnant, the same venue where my waters had broken with Brooke. When I was on stage I could feel that something wasn't right. I was near the end of my set and when I went to the toilet afterwards noticed I was bleeding really heavily; I was terrified I was losing the baby. Thankfully Craig was with me at that gig, so I went to find him and he took me straight to hospital. By the time we got there it was late and there was no one available to do my scan, so I went back the following morning to get properly checked over. I cannot even begin to tell you how relieved I was when they said that the baby was okay. Sadly they did say that the loss of blood I'd experienced may have potentially been a twin. It was very sad to think about what might have been but I'll probably never know what actually happened and I was so grateful that there was still a healthy baby inside of me.

After that scare I scaled everything back. I knew that I needed to take things easy and it would have been really hard for me to carry on gigging like I had in the past. Because Brooke had been so premature I had to go to the Prem Prevention Clinic at the Leicester General for scans and to be monitored regularly. Craig wanted me to rest as much as possible, so I became very familiar with daytime TV.

When it was time for the 20-week scan Craig and I were both desperate to find out the sex of the baby as we had done with Brooke. Craig was insisting he didn't mind whether it was a boy or girl, but as soon as the nurse told us we were having a boy his face broke into a massive grin. We went straight to Toys R Us and bought Brooke a present and the first few bits for our son. When my dad was ill he'd said to me, 'Sam, if you ever have a boy, will you name him Tommy?' I was going to be called Tommy if I was a boy and my dad had an Uncle Tommy he thought the world of, so it was a name that meant a lot to him. My due date was 7th June – my dad's birthday, so it felt only right that we should honour his wishes. From then on whenever we talked about my bump we called him Tommy and it felt right.

Poor Brooke wasn't all that happy about the fact she was going to have a little brother. She'd always said she wanted a sister to play with, so when we told her it was a boy she burst into tears. We had to try and placate her with a Peppa Pig toy but she kept crying and saying, 'I don't want a brother, I want a sister. I don't like boys.' We kept telling her what an amazing big sister she was going to be to little Tommy but she still wasn't keen!

Two weeks before my due date I was booked in for a blood test at my local doctors. I was talking to one of nurses and I started getting this pulling sensation in my tummy. The nurse said it was probably Braxton Hicks – practice contractions, or Toni Braxton's as I used to call them – but by the time I'd got back home it was much worse. It kept tightening and then stopping and my neighbour Yvonne said to me, 'Sam, I think you're in labour.' I called the Leicester Royal Infirmary hospital and because Brooke was early they asked me to go straight down there. Craig's mum came over to look after Brooke and Craig and I headed off. I took my birthing bag just in case, but I thought they'd probably be sending me back home within the hour. How wrong was I!

I was hooked up to a machine which monitors your contractions and the nurse told me they were less than five minutes apart. The doctor came in and did some other tests and told me I had to stay in hospital. That's when it hit me that I could be having my baby that day. I was about to send Craig off with a list of things I wanted, like magazines and munchies, but as I rolled out of the bed to say goodbye it felt like a water balloon popped in my stomach and my waters broke all over the floor. The nurse told me it would be a little while before I was ready to go into the delivery room and told Craig he could go back home for a while and pick up the stuff I wanted.

Craig left and I settled down to watch *Britain's Got Talent* but all of a sudden I felt a pain like I'd never felt before. I shot up in bed and I could barely breathe. By the time the nurse came in I was screaming and crying and everyone else on the ward was staring at me. I was so embarrassed. The nurse called Craig and he came straight back to the hospital and got there just as they were wheeling me upstairs to the delivery suite. I was biting the bed sheet to stop myself screaming and the nurse quickly gave me gas and air. I hadn't experienced any of that pain with Brooke, so I honestly had no idea how intense it could be. I think Craig thought I'd turned into some kind of monster. He came over to comfort me and I was shouting at him, saying, 'You did this! It's all your fault!'

Then suddenly I felt really calm and had a happy moment and I started singing Whitney songs. I was switching between screaming and crying and then laughing and singing every few minutes. I was completely delirious and didn't know what I was doing or saying. At one point I said to one of the nurses, 'You do know who I am don't you?' I wasn't *anyone*! I was inviting people to my wedding, and obviously I'd already got married, and I also said I hoped the baby wasn't ginger because my brother got bullied for being a redhead when he was a kid. I was off my head on the gas and air and my head was all over the place.

Finally the anesthetist came in and gave me an epidural. Afterwards I told her she should have an award – and then

I invited her to my wedding too! Within seconds the pain had gone and for the next four hours I sat on the bed playing with my DS and everything was silent and chilled out. Then it all started again... At about midnight my contractions really kicked in and I knew the baby was coming. The nurse said I could start pushing and suddenly I heard someone say, 'We can see the head!' This little baby came out that looked like a little floppy chicken. I panicked slightly and then I heard a high-pitched, powerful cry. Tommy had arrived!

He was 5lb 13oz. The midwife put him in a cot next to me and he was so adorable. I didn't have any problems with breastfeeding him at all and things seemed to be going really smoothly. Well, until I attempted to go to the toilet. I'd been stitched up and no one told me I was supposed to pour warm water as I was weeing to dilute the acidity. I started to go and I absolutely screamed my head off. A nurse came running in and opened the door from the outside. I was floods of tears; it was agony. I won't ever make that mistake again.

I was allowed to take Tommy home the following morning, so Craig came to collect us and the first thing I heard was Brooke running up the corridor to the ward. As soon as she saw Tommy she was stroking his head and kissing him. I think she soon forgot about not wanting a baby brother! Back home we had tons of visitors over the next few days, but I was exhausted. I was having trouble sleeping and my boobs started to go really hard. At one point I was leaning over the sink with them in ice-cold water to try and soothe them. When the health visitor came round she checked me over and said I had mastitis and sent me straight to bed. Tommy had to go onto powdered milk for a while, which I hated, but I had no choice because I was put on antibiotics. I felt like I was really on the edge and scared I was on the brink of postnatal depression. I didn't want to do anything or see anyone. I just wanted to sleep all the time.

Tommy's crying was keeping me awake constantly, but then every time he stopped crying I would panic and think there was something wrong with him. Craig was amazing and he kept making up bottles and feeding him, but on top of everything else Tommy kept getting ill. He always had quite a high temperature and he was crying but the doctor couldn't find anything wrong with him. That carried on for several months and it was a massive worry. I remember going to check on Tommy one night and he was sat up in his cot choking and his face had tuned blue. He'd been sick and it had got stuck in his throat. Craig rang 999 and he was diagnosed with gastroenteritis. We couldn't understand why he was so unwell all the time. Shortly afterwards we discovered that it was because he was having a really bad reaction to the formula, which we stopped immediately.

We had several other health scares with Tommy when he was a toddler. One time I was changing his nappy when he was about two years old, I noticed that one of his testicles was much bigger than the other one. I took him to the doctor and he said it could be a strangulated hernia, which could potentially have killed him if left untreated. He was admitted to hospital and we were told that because he'd been sick so much he'd damaged the tube inside one of his testicles; it was filling up with fluid but it wasn't draining. It happened several times after that, so we were constantly in and out of hospital with him.

When Tommy got a bit older I started doing a few gigs here and there to make some extra cash. I was doing a show in a club in Birmingham with Showaddywaddy and Frank Carson and when I got off stage I had a load of missed calls from Craig and messages saying that Tommy had been taken back into hospital. I hadn't even had time to take my PA system down after I'd performed, but within five minutes the other acts had done it for me and sent me on my way. Showaddywaddy and Frank really helped me out and without them I would have felt even more panicked.

Driving from Birmingham to the hospital was one of the most horrific journeys I've ever had to do. The hospital staff were amazing but I was at my wits' end. Tommy was checked over and monitored overnight and he was diagnosed with gastroenteritis. Whenever Tommy had been ill it was so hard to get him eating again because he went right off his food. As a result he was a tiny little thing and I was constantly worrying about him. I ended up taking him to a dietician when he was about a year and a half old because he wouldn't eat anything. The dietician's advice was to sit him in his high chair, let him eat with his hands and not to make any fuss at mealtimes. From then on, every time we were out in a restaurant people used to look at me with disgust. I guess to them it looked like I was letting my son eat with his hands and totally ignoring him, but it's what I had been *told* to do. We went through a real difficult time with him because, of course, we knew he had to eat to survive, but he just wasn't interested in food for so long. Tommy didn't eat with a spoon until he was about three, and then Sunday dinners became his favourite meal so we'd have those as often as possible. Sunday dinners became Monday dinners, Tuesday dinners, and so on. He's so much better now and he likes food a lot more, which makes things so much easier. Unfortunately, like most kids he also loves pizza and burgers now, but he does still love a roast.

After my disastrous first *X Factor* audition, my second ill-fated foray into the world of TV talent shows was when I applied for *Britain's Got Talent* in 2010. I went to Birmingham Hippodrome and queued up for hours. Brooke had begged to come with me, so she was my wing woman. I sang 'Take Another Little Piece of My Heart' by Janis Joplin, but I think Brooke got more screen time than me because she was so cute. I didn't get past the first round; it was a bit of a blow getting another knockback but it clearly just wasn't my time. I felt like I'd been really brave trying out for another show after my previous failure and now it had happened again. Maybe talent shows just weren't for me.

I'd put the prison service on the backburner after I had Tommy because I was so busy looking after him, but in 2010 I got an email from a woman who worked for HMP Shared Services, which is the main customer services department of the prison service. It had been almost 18 months since I'd done my Recruitment Assessment Day and a job had come up at HMP Gartree. It was out of the blue but I knew straight away that I wanted to do it. I had to do the fitness test again, but I passed no problem and went on to Prison Service College in Rugby to complete my six weeks training. It was about a 25-minute journey from my house and they wanted everyone to stay during the week and only go home at weekends, but I wasn't comfortable with that. Because I had the kids, I came home every night, and then I'd do my revision and drive back each morning. We had exams at the end of the six weeks and if you failed those you couldn't join the prison service full stop, so I was studying really hard. We learnt everything from first aid to equality to understanding radicalisation. Even though it was a long slog, it was a brilliant course, and well worth all the hard work I'd put in when I found out I'd passed all of the assessments. I had a passing-out parade where I got to collect my diploma. Craig, my mum and Brooke came along to watch the ceremony, and by the end of the day I was officially a prison officer.

I was starting work the following week. It was tricky to

juggle everything. Brooke was in reception class, but Tommy had to be looked after by a childminder. I found a local lady we'll call Janice. She seemed really nice and I liked that her house backed onto a park so she could take the kids out in the fresh air. The toys she had were very old and I even had to take my own crayons round for Tommy to play with, so it wasn't the perfect situation, but she seemed caring and professional and that was the most important thing.

My first day as a prison officer was nerve-wracking. I'd watched all kinds of scary things about prisons on TV and even though I'd been taught how to handle all kinds of different situations, I hadn't had any first-hand experience of them yet. I was wearing my uniform and my epaulettes so I looked the part, but now I had to crack on and actually do the job.

I remember walking down one of the wings for the first time and some of the prisoners said hello to me and were very respectful. I definitely wasn't a civvy any more; I was now a screw. I was still learning the ropes for the first few weeks, so I just observed the other officers and shadowed them. I didn't have keys and I wasn't allowed to restrain someone if there was an incident. I just had to watch and learn. It was quite frustrating because I wanted to get involved but it was important for me to get to know my colleagues and learn how to fill out all of the forms – of which there were many.

When I first started work I was just a basic prison officer. The inmates I looked after had things they had to do every day, like go to work, go on courses or go to AA. The ones who were unemployed or not doing courses were locked up in their cells all day. They didn't all hang out playing snooker and having a laugh like they do on prison shows. That's a bit of a fallacy.

It wasn't a case of officers versus inmates either. We worked *with* them. If there were problems we'd tried to help them, and if they were up to no good we'd have to try and get them back on the straight and narrow. Some days I'd patrol the landings, and others I'd be in the workshops or in the yard at exercise times. Sometimes things got a bit menacing. For instance, if a bell went off because someone was on suicide watch or they'd set fire to their cell, I would assist. Those things didn't happen that often but they did happen.

H Wing, where I worked, became a Psychological Informed Planned Environment, also known as a PIPE Wing. Quite a lot of prisons have them now and they're for prisoners who have done anger-management or healthy-relationship courses. These are quite high-intensity courses that prisoners have to do as part of their sentences in order to progress and move on. Some of the courses take up to a year, but once they've completed them the prisoners can come onto the PIPE Wing.

My job changed with the move, and a big part of it became about observing the prisoners and doing group sessions. Our direct bosses were psychologists and we'd follow their instructions and then write reports. If we saw that someone was getting into an argument with another prisoner, we'd watch to see how they handled it. If they dealt with it in the way they'd learnt to on the courses we'd speak to them about what went right, or if they dealt with the situation badly we'd discuss better ways to go about things. I wasn't just a prison officer with a set of keys; I was working very closely with certain offenders.

I was a personal officer to some prisoners, which is where you are given around eight to twelve prisoners to look after who will come to you first if they've got problems. That meant I had to sit down and talk through their lives with them, right back to how they were treated as a child. It was all about getting to the core of their problems and trying to understand what made them do the things they did. We helped them to change their thought patterns and it was amazing when you could see a really positive switch in someone. We couldn't change their pasts but through the work we did we could help them to change their futures.

Like all prisons, it was full of a real cross-section of prisoners who had committed all kinds of crimes. People often ask if I was scared doing the job but if ever anything kicked off, adrenalin took over. I always knew I was working in an environment that was safe. If an alarm bell ever went off, within a matter of minutes you'd have 20 officers on the scene dealing with the situation. Quite a lot of hairy things went on but I never once felt like I was in real danger.

When the summer holidays arrived, Brooke started going

along to the childminder with Tommy while I was at work. I came home one evening and Craig told me that Brooke had been found playing on train tracks with two other boys who were being looked after by Janice. They'd gone outside to play and she hadn't even noticed that they'd left the green, crossed the road and walked through an alleyway to the train tracks. The boys had taken Brooke down there and she said that even though she knew it was wrong, she'd been too scared to snitch on them. After she went to bed I sat on the sofa and sobbed. I was so upset that my little girl had been put in danger. I decided there and then that neither of my children would ever be looked after by that woman again. I immediately emailed Ofsted and reported Janice. She didn't even have permission for my child to be outside of her house without her. That's not what you call 'minding' a child.

I phoned another local childminder I knew called Laura and hearing how upset I was she invited me round. As soon as I saw how lovely her house was I didn't even think about the cost; I was just so relieved that I'd found somewhere so clean and modern and warm. Both of the kids loved going to Laura's from day one and it made me feel so much happier leaving them each day.

I didn't put on as much weight when I was pregnant with Tommy as with Brooke, but it also didn't come off as quickly, which I was fine about. I knew I was never going to be the rake I was when I was younger and I didn't give myself a hard time about it. I was about a size 12 by the time I started at HMP Gartree and I felt pretty comfortable.

Apart from when I was pregnant, I'd smoked non-stop since I was 15. But one day I saw my daughter copy me smoking using a candy stick. I put my fag out there and then and I haven't touched one since. She was only six and I was completely horrified. I went cold turkey from that moment on. Craig did the same, and not surprisingly we wanted to kill each other for two weeks, but it was so worth it.

Of course one of the side effects of giving up smoking is the weight gain. Every time I wanted a cigarette I'd have a bar of chocolate instead and in a matter of months I ballooned to a size 16–18. I had to keep going to the prison uniform department to get bigger shirts and trousers. I even started wearing men's trousers because the women's were too tight. I felt so self-conscious that even in the height of summer I wore a zipped up jacket at all times because my boobs were so big I wanted to cover them up. It didn't help that I was working with a large group of men. I was so hot all the time and it was horrible.

It didn't cross my mind to go on a diet because I'd never been on one in my life. I don't understand the concept of salad. I may as well just go into the garden and eat grass as eat cress. The only time I'd ever eat lettuce is in a cheese sandwich, and even then I'd have really strong Cheddar to disguise the taste. All the other officers were going off to the prison gym at lunchtime to work out, but all I wanted to do was watch *Loose Women*, have a cup of tea and eat biscuits and crisps.

We had different shifts, so sometimes I didn't get home until 8pm and I'd have been up since 6am. I'd have dinner, usually a pizza, watch a bit of TV and then go to bed. I used to skip breakfast and then stop at the garage on the way to work and buy a newspaper and cakes and biscuits for everyone. Oh, and some sweets for me to have in my pocket during the day. I was eating so much rubbish and also eating at the wrong times. The pounds went on so quickly I didn't even really notice to start with, and by the time I realised how big I'd got I felt like it was too late to do anything about it.

What I wore out of work totally changed too. I started wearing Craig's jumpers and T-shirts because they were the only things that fitted me. I worked every other weekend and when I was at home I'd either want to play with the kids or I'd be catching up with TV. Craig and I hardly saw each other during that time and we were always shattered. We were both working so much we didn't have much of a social life, so I didn't really bother with make-up and I never bought myself new clothes. What was the point when I had nowhere to wear them?

CHAPTER 9

ONE MOMENT
IN TIME

I applied to *The X Factor* in 2013 completely on a whim. We always watched the show and in the break an advert came up saying, 'Would you like to be on *The X Factor*? Apply now!' I thought, sod it, I know it didn't exactly go well last time but I've got nothing to lose. The kids love the show and they know what's going on now they're a bit older, and I would love to make them proud. I filled out the application form on my iPad and whispered the news to Craig so that the kids didn't know.

I wasn't in the best place because I still felt really big and frumpy, but I missed performing and at that time I couldn't see another way to try and break into the industry. I was enjoying being a prison officer and if it was what I ended up doing for the rest of my life then so be it, but I had to give singing one last go.

Just after I applied I had a bit of a windfall thanks to a PPI claim, so that April Craig and I booked to take the kids to Florida on holiday. In Hollywood Studios in Disney World they had a competition called the American Idol Experience. I thought it would be a laugh to enter, and the kids would get to see me sing. I was wearing shorts, a T-shirt and flip-flops, so I didn't look terribly glamorous, but I must have done something right because I kept getting through the heats into the next round. By the end of the day there were five of us in the final with 3,000 people watching. I sang 'Get Here' by Oleta Adams and ended up winning the whole bloody thing! I was given a golden ticket that enabled you to jump the queue and go straight to the Bootcamp stage of *American Idol* on TV. When I was walking around the park afterwards people were asking for my autograph and having photos taken with me and all sorts. It was so bizarre. It's incredible to look back now and realise that none of those people would have known I would go on to win *The X Factor* in the UK.

Because I wasn't American I wasn't allowed to use the golden ticket, but I managed to track down the lad who came second in the competition, a lovely guy called Jesse Cline. I gave it to him and he ended up getting really far in the competition. In fact, while he was appearing on *American Idol*, I was on *The X Factor* over here.

A few days into the holiday I checked my emails and I had one from *The X Factor* UK saying: 'Congratulations. You've got an audition on 12th April'. We were flying home on the 11th and it was Craig's 40th on the 12th, so we were having a massive party at the house. The timing could have been better (seriously, what *is* it with me and bad timing?). Thankfully I was able to rearrange the date, but it meant I had to go all the way to Cardiff to audition.

The week after we came back from Florida I headed down to the Motorpoint Arena in Cardiff. I'd been in the queue all day when one of the researchers, a guy called Ollie, came over and started talking to me. I was still heavy at the time and I was telling him about how I used to be a size ten and now felt like a heifer. I explained that the reason I'd shied away from trying out for so long was because I was so self-conscious. There were other people in the queue who looked like models and I felt like this bloated mess. I told him all about working in the prison service and my life back in Leicester, and he frantically wrote everything down.

When I eventually got to perform, I sang 'Who's Loving You' by The Jacksons, and when I finished everyone started clapping and I was handed a ticket, which meant I was through to the next round. I wanted to jump up and down I was so happy. I had to go for another audition that day, and then they asked me to go back the following day to sing for the executive producers. I sang 'Who's Loving You' again, and a bit of 'Run To You' by Whitney Houston. When I finished they were very straight-faced and said casually, 'We'll let you know.' That was it. I was convinced I was out and headed back to Leicester feeling really despondent.

Life went on as normal. I went back to the prison service and tried to forget all about *The X Factor*; in my mind I'd failed again. I was leaving work around six weeks later and when I turned on my phone Ollie the researcher had left me a message saying, 'Sam, great news. We've got you an audition this Thursday at the Excel in London. Can you make it?' I thought it would be another audition in front of the researchers or producers because they have so many people to get through before putting together the shortlist in front of the real judges. But no. This time I was going to be performing in front of Sharon, Louis, Nicole and Gary. I frantically rang Craig to tell him the news, and the next day at work I was begging people to cover my shift the following day so I could go to London. Thankfully someone stepped up and offered to swap a day with me, and even the governor of the prison wished me good luck!

Craig and I were up ridiculously early on the Thursday to drive to London in Craig's little van. I didn't really think about the audition too much on the journey. I'm not one to overthink things and worry until I really need to. I always leave things to the last minute, even if it's learning the lyrics to a song. I'll have a last-minute panic but it always gets done. I think I work better under pressure.

We had to be there for 7am and when we were waiting in the queue, we got chatting to a band called Next of Kin and their family and friends. We ended up in the waiting room with them and I was fascinated because they'd been through it all before when they were younger, so they were telling me about how the music industry works and how tough it can be. I knew a bit about the business thanks to being on the club circuit, but it was nothing compared to what they'd experienced.

They'd been on the brink of being massive back in the *Smash Hits* era and then it had all gone horribly wrong for them. They wanted to make it so much and I felt so bad for them. Their audition was amazing and they can really sing. They performed a song their mum had written and it was unbelievable. I absolutely love those boys and we're still in touch now. I've even got a Next of Kin T-shirt that I wear to bed!

I also met another lovely lad called Tom Mann, who was a part-time football coach, and a load of the kids he coaches had come along with him. He was such a nice lad and he was a bit different because he played the guitar when he performed. I thought he was really talented too.

As Craig and I sat in the waiting room, I joked about wanting to sing with Gary Barlow. Who wouldn't? But I did also add that he wasn't as nice as Craig. I didn't want to make him feel insecure when I was about to meet one of the country's biggest heart-throbs (and I don't mean Louis). I also talked about how I felt, at 35, that this was my last shot at a singing career. And I meant it. It's so hard to break into the industry anyway, but when you're an overweight woman over 35 who's been knocked back a couple of times it feels harder than ever. But as I said at the time, you've at least got to try. I knew that day could completely change my life.

Every time the cameras came round to film me I seemed to be eating. Mainly pretzels. Dermot came over to do an interview with me and he was really lovely and chatty. After several hours, I was finally called in to see the judges. I was bloody petrified walking into that room. Even though there were lots of members of the crew in there, it felt quiet and empty because all I could see were the four judges looking at me. I felt and looked hideous. I was wearing black harem trousers with heels and a green snakeskin top. It was the only thing I had in my wardrobe that was vaguely smart because I never went out. It was also the only thing I could fit into and felt comfortable in. Wearing heels is always a big thing for me because I can't walk in them to save my life. I'm a bit bow-legged and I'm always worried that I'm going to look like Whoopi Goldberg in *Ghost*. It was okay when I was doing the clubs because I was just standing in the corner of a room and I would usually walk on in heels and then take them off after one song. No one noticed because they were usually half-cut. I'd washed my hair and left it to dry naturally, so it was really curly, and I had hardly any make-up on. I think it's safe to say I don't do glamour unless someone else is doing it for me!

I was so overwhelmed to be there and I still couldn't quite believe that I was standing in front of the *real* judges. Literally feet away from me were music mogul Louis Walsh, Sharon Osbourne, who's been in the business for years and is an absolute legend, Gary Barlow, who is basically amazing, and Nicole Scherzinger, who is so stunning and talented. I felt like I either wanted to leg it out of the room as fast as I could or pray the floor would open and swallow me up. I was so intimidated.

Sharon spoke to me first: she loved the fact I was a prison officer and asked if I put handcuffs on people. I said I did but not pink fluffy ones! Sharon then asked me if my dream was to sing, and of course I said yes. Then it was time for me to do my to audition. And breathe... It felt like it took an age for my backing music to start, but once it did I just went for it.

I chose to perform 'Listen' by Beyoncé because there was a girl at my American Idol Experience audition who sang it. I'd never really heard it before and I thought it was amazing. It's ironic that I got the chance to support Beyoncé as part of my winner's package all those months later.

That particular song was also almost like a statement, because I'd been singing for so many years and no one had ever *really* listened. My voice had been really strong for about four or five years, ever since I'd branched out on my own and started to sing lots of different types of songs. I had my own PA system and I had freedom but no one had really stood up and noticed and told me I had talent. I desperately wanted some recognition. I also wanted it to be about my voice. I didn't want to be judged on how I looked and for people to just see a mum or a wife or a prison officer.

I stood there, closed my eyes and gave it my best shot. I tried not to look at the judges because I didn't want them to see how petrified I was. I didn't want anyone to feel sorry for me. Your eyes are the windows to your soul, they say, so people can really see hurt or anything else you're struggling with. About halfway through the song I sneaked a peak at the judges and I could see them all looking at each other as if to say '*WHAT*?' In my head I kept thinking, 'I hope I'm doing alright.' When it came to the end of the song the last note sounded awful, and as I belted it out I thought I'd totally cocked it up. I was cross with myself.

When I finished I realised that all of the judges were on their feet giving me a standing ovation. It's hard to put into words how amazing that felt. I was so emotional and I was trying so hard not to break down. I found out later it was the first standing ovation all of the judges had given, and they were nearly at the end of the auditions. Wow.

Louis said he wasn't expecting me to sound like that at all. Nicole was gobsmacked and said I sang the song exactly how it should have been sung. Gary spoke next and said that my voice was incredible. It was all too much for me and I got *really* teary, especially knowing that Craig was outside watching everything. I got four 'yeses' and I was so overwhelmed I ran out of the room to see Craig (not easy for me in heels). He gave me a massive hug and half of me was crying and the other half was embarrassed that so much attention was on me.

Everyone in the waiting room started clapping me and it was so surreal. Craig said that as soon as I started singing, the entire waiting room went quiet. I was so happy that I'd been myself. I hadn't tried to be anything I wasn't with cool clothes and loads of make-up. I'd stayed true to myself and the judges liked it. It felt like a real validation that I was okay. My husband looked the other day, and the video of my audition has had 11 million views or something ridiculous on YouTube. It does make me wonder whether I should have worn something a bit more glam, but I think I would have looked and felt even *more* uncomfortable.

The first thing I did was phone the kids to tell them I'd got through, and they were so excited it set me off and I burst into tears again. Those moments will be etched on my mind forever. Every time I watch the video back – which isn't often, I might add – I really pick at it. There are so many bits I wish I could go back and change. I came in too early on the song, for a start. The first 'listen' should have been much later and I knew straight away I'd done it wrong. I don't know if the judges realised, and I had to carry on and pretend nothing was wrong, but inside I was dying.

After that, I was whisked off all over the place to do interviews and I didn't even get a chance to eat because things were so manic. I was expecting to be at home by 6pm having egg and chips and seeing the kids, but because my audition caused a bit of a stir I didn't get home until really late. Craig and I did a Maccy D's run on the way back; I think that was our first conversation after my audition, actually – what to have for dinner. After we left the Excel we both sat in silence for about half an hour driving up the M1, both of us thinking 'Did that really just happen?' It had been non-stop and that was the first chance we got to really take everything in and process it.

I was told that the next round would be in front of 4,000 people at Wembley arena. Oh. My. God. That was going to be the biggest crowd I'd ever performed in front of. I needed some new clothes desperately! I knew my hoodies and jeans wouldn't cut it. I had to ask friends to come shopping with me and help me out because I was so clueless. I felt like a Weeble in everything.

Craig and I talked about what I would sing and I felt *so* nervous. We went back and forth with so many different ideas but in the end I decided to sing The Jackson's 'Who's Loving You' like I had done in my first audition. It was a song that meant a lot to me because I used to perform it back when I was a teenager. It may sound a bit crazy but people used to tell me I sounded like Michael Jackson when I sang it, and I knew it was a song I could really belt out.

Now I knew I was going through to the next round I had to let work know what was happening. I hadn't shouted from the rooftops about my audition, so not that many people knew about it. I hadn't told any of the prisoners at that point, but I knew it was going to be televised so they were definitely going to find out eventually – even if I didn't make it past the Wembley audition. I explained the situation to the governors and I had to get confirmation that I could take time off, which luckily they were brilliant about.

By the time the arena audition rolled around in July 2013, I'd hit 36. We were allowed to take as many people along with us as we wanted, and of course everyone and their dog wanted to come. I was particular about who I took along, though. I didn't want people who were just there for the ride: I wanted people who were a support and had been there for me. There were a few people that kind of came out of the woodwork after years and wanted a piece of the action and I ruffled a few feathers because I said a few couldn't come. It had become quite draining and I didn't want my 'entourage' to be the focus of the day. I would happily have just had my closest family and friends but in the end there were about 20 of us, and that was more than enough.

My friend Karen works for a printing firm so we got T-shirts made up for my kids saying 'Sam Bailey's daughter' and 'Sam Bailey's son' with the *X Factor* logo on the front. When other people saw them they all wanted them too, so the majority of people who came along were wearing a 'Sam Bailey' top.

I had to be at the audition really early and it was mad being at Wembley knowing I was going to be singing on the same stage that so many world famous singers had performed on. It just happened to be one of the hottest days I've ever experienced. I was wearing harem trousers again, this time with a leopard-print sleeveless top and some sandals. I still felt like a fat mum, and the little bit of make-up I'd put on had sweated off on the drive up, so I must have looked a right state.

There were so many people waiting outside the venue to see the judges and they wished me good luck as I went in. It was all new to me and it felt weird that people were pulling me from pillar to post and fussing over me. I was starting to recognise people who had auditioned for the show before, and that felt really big time because I knew they'd been there in previous years. The website Digital Spy had already printed information about who was good and who was standing out at the early auditions and they'd named me. Someone must have been tipping them off. I was pleased they'd name-checked me, but it also felt quite scary because now I had to live up to the hype.

It was *such* a long, busy day and people were running around manically with clipboards and radios. We were waiting backstage for ages; the crew had cordoned off about half of the arena and there were boxes for us to sit on. There was also a make-up area. The camera crew were filming people getting ready in the mirrors and they asked if I wanted to go and join them and be filmed and I was like, 'Erm, this is as good as it gets! I won't be putting on any more make-up on today. This is me.' My kids loved it. They got to meet Louis, and Nicole came and had her photo taken with them, and I think it will probably always be one of the best days of their lives.

My mother-in-law was with us and she's got fibromyalgia so she can't stand for too long, and my sister-in-law was about six months pregnant. My friend Christine was also in a wheelchair and I was so worried about all of them. Making sure the kids had enough juice and everyone had drinks helped to take my mind off what I was about to do. Every time someone went out and performed you could hear the screams from the audience and it would stop me in my tracks and remind me where I was and what I was doing.

Just before I went on stage Dermot came over to have a chat and it was so funny to see all of my friends and family packing in tightly around me so they could get on TV. Tommy was having a whale of a time with Dermot. They became best buddies. Dermot was so taken aback by how much Tommy looked like him when he was a kid. They were pinching each other's noses and playing and it was so sweet. Dermot is one of the nicest guys you'll ever meet.

I felt like I'd been there for days and done a million interviews when the time came for me to perform. I was standing at the side of the stage watching Kingsland Road, and then it was my turn. I felt so aware of myself walking out onto the stage. Thankfully I didn't have heels on but there wasn't even a hint of ladylikeness in the way I walked over to the mic. Gary said, 'Oh, here she comes!' and I gave him a quick smile. I introduced myself to the audience and told them what I did for a living and loads of people cheered, but there were definitely a couple of boos too.

I started singing and I properly went for it. My bolshiness came out as I moved around the stage. I'm not a dainty hand-moving kind of person, I'm a definite fist puncher, and I was doing that all the way. I had my eyes closed and when I opened them everyone in the arena was on their feet. It was amazing. In that moment I didn't care what happened afterwards because I'd got what I came for. I'd got recognition and it felt unbelievable. I would have died a happy woman there and then.

After I sang 'Who's Loving' the judges joked that they felt like they were at a Sam Bailey concert and then said they wanted to hear another song. I performed 'Run To You' by Whitney Houston and that song has always reminded me of my dad. There have been so many times where I've wanted to run up and give him a hug but he's not around anymore, so it was really emotive for me. I liked to think he was watching me from somewhere, giving me a measured nod and saying it was 'handsome'.

When I finished, the judges said that they could have sat there and listened to me all day, and they all said they wanted to see me at the next stage. I mean, seriously? One day I was working in the prison service, and the next I was performing for music legends and 4,000 members of the public, including some of my family and closest friends. Who does that? Up until that point I wouldn't have said it was 'Sam Bailey from Leicester'.

I could see someone running towards me from the corner of my eye and when I turned around it was Brooke with a massive smile on her face. Tommy was sound asleep in Craig's arms, and my mother-in-law ran on without her wheelchair. It was like she was magically cured! We did take the mickey out of her something terrible afterwards. She has good days and bad days and she can't stand for long, but somehow she managed to leg it on stage and give me a hug that day!

I was absolutely buzzing when I got off stage and I went straight off to do some interviews. It was after I'd finished them that I discovered the power of Twitter. I already had a Twitter account under the name Sammy Soprano, but I only had about 60 followers. I searched my name and so many comments came up saying things like 'look out for her, she's going to be the winner'. It freaked me out a bit to see the public talking about me. I was officially a little bit 'known'.

I changed my name to Sam Bailey on Twitter and I got more followers that day as a result. I've now got over 350,000 followers, so I'm much more careful about what I say. I had to deactivate my Facebook account because people started taking private photos off it, and when that happened it was a whole new world. My life changed so quickly.

I was so chuffed that I'd gone through to Bootcamp, but there was one little problem. Every year on 2nd January I book a holiday for the family to go away, and I'd arranged for us all to go to Haven at Devon Cliffs with my mum. I'd paid for it all upfront and we were due to go in early August for a week. On the way home I turned to Craig and said, 'Shit! Holiday! Bootcamp is the same week.' I didn't want to cancel it because the kids were really looking forward to it, so I told Craig that he'd have to go with my mum. You can imagine how well that went down.

Even though things were being leaked on the Internet, we had to keep the fact I'd got through to Bootcamp as quiet as possible, which meant the kids couldn't even tell their friends. That was hard for them because they were so excited. And I won't lie; it was quite hard for me too. I wanted to tell the world.

The other issue was work, because of course I had to tell my bosses I was through to Bootcamp. I had booked the week off because of the holiday anyway, but we had to talk about the 'what ifs'. 'What if' I got through Bootcamp and had to go to Judges' Houses? 'What if' I got into the live finals? The governor of the prison was really supportive and sweet about it all. I didn't think he was going to turn around and say my job was on the line if I carried on in the show because he's a really nice guy, but there was always a slight risk he would say that me being in the show was too disruptive when it came to the prison. He would have had every right to feel that way.

Bootcamp was looming and I had a lot of my mind. Once again, one of the main things being 'What the hell am I going to wear?' I still didn't own many clothes and we were going to be there for six days. I borrowed some money from my friend Jo so I could go shopping and I took my sister-in-law Laura along with me so she could give me fashion advice. I really needed something decent to wear on stage. I knew that everyone would be upping their game. I bought some Ted Baker sandals, some linen trousers and a load of tops. River Island proved to be a bit of a goldmine for bits and I spoilt myself with a couple of tops from All Saints as well.

Bootcamp was held at Wembley Arena and we were all booked in to stay at the Premier Inn in Wembley Park. We pretty much took the hotel over. I went down to London a day early with a girl called Katy and a guy called Lee that I knew from the gigging circuit. They'd got through to Bootcamp too, and we went around London for a day of fun and then shared a hotel room that night. The rest of the contestants turned up the next day with their suitcases and the show filmed us walking down the concourse to the arena. There were hundreds of us and we had to walk up and down loads of times to get the best shot. It was knackering!

Just after we got back to the hotel I got a phone call from my Auntie Jo who told me that my nan didn't have long to live. She had lung cancer, which I was very aware of, but she deteriorated really quickly. Jo told me she probably only had days left. I was very upset but I made the decision not to tell anyone else who was at Bootcamp. I didn't want it to become a 'story'. I didn't want to be 'Sam, who's doing it for her nan'. It was a private situation.

We were given the information about who we were sharing rooms with and the same day found out who our mentors would be. We all had to stand outside and wait for the limos with the judges inside to pull up. I was praying I'd get Sharon, because I loved her from the minute I met her, or Gary, because he's a real singers' singer. The Girls' category mentor was revealed first and we just saw this incredible leg emerge from the back of a car followed by Nicole. It was the Overs turn next, my group, and when I saw Sharon's amazing heel step out of the car I burst into tears and went running towards her. You can see me sobbing on the footage. I hadn't had a proper chance to meet her yet and I had so much respect for her. I was laughing and crying at the same time.

Next we were sent off to learn our group songs. I was put into a group with two women called Katie and Shelley, who appeared on the live finals. Shelley is this big bubble of loveliness that you can't help but laugh at. She was full-on, but I thought she was great. We had a choice of three songs and we had to decide which one we liked most. We decided on 'I'm Every Woman' by Chaka Khan and I felt slightly sorry for Katie because she had a real Rod Stewart husk to her voice and so it wasn't an easy one for her. I was worried we'd made the wrong choice on the song and I wanted Katie to feel comfortable, but she insisted we went ahead. We worked really hard and it helped to take my mind off my nan. The thought that she could potentially pass away that day was horrifying.

It was a really long day and we were all exhausted and ready for bed. The hotel bar was full of people partying, and all of the corridors were packed with others rehearsing. I just wanted to go to sleep but when we got into bed we discovered that our sheets were damp. My pyjamas were getting wet and it was really uncomfortable. We called reception and asked them to change them but, awfully, one of the other contestants had collapsed and an ambulance had been called so they were understandably manic. As a result it, took an hour and a half for someone to come and change our sheets, by which time I was practically falling asleep standing up. I was cold, damp and exhausted. By the time we finally climbed into bed I was so overtired I couldn't sleep.

The following day I was beyond tired, but I had to pull myself together because we had a full-on day ahead. I had breakfast with Shelley; she'd been sharing with a slightly bonkers woman who had kept her awake until 3am, so she was feeling pretty rubbish too. Just before we performed Shelley started crying. She was worried that her voice wasn't up to scratch because she was so shattered. When we got onto the stage Shelley told the judges that she hadn't had any sleep. I kept quiet because I've never been to a concert where someone said they're tired or their voice wasn't feeling great. You just have to get on with it. I don't think the people who were coming out with excuses did themselves any favours. I could easily have told the judges that we'd had a late night because of the bed sheets but I didn't want to try and go for the sympathy vote. What I didn't know was that one of my roommates had done exactly that earlier in the day. She'd told the judges that she was tired and that she'd been sharing with me, and it had been noted that I didn't try and use our bed nightmare as an excuse.

We all really went for it but I thought I'd totally buggered things up. Sharon gave Katie and I a bit of a pep talk and said that the competition was dog eat dog and we were up against each other. I learnt a valid lesson that day. It may seem selfish but at the end of the day you're there for you, so you have to concentrate on that.

Thankfully we did all get 'yeses', so we were through to the next round. What a relief. There were 12 of us in the Over-25s category, but there were only six seats on the stage. If you performed well you got to take a seat, but if there were more than six of you that had nailed it the judges would start swapping people around and you could lose your place to go forward into the Judges' Houses round.

I was going to sing 'Take Another Little Piece of My Heart' by Janis Joplin, but I changed it at the last minute and I sang 'Clown' by Emeli Sandé instead. It felt like a pertinent song to sing. All that was going through my head at Bootcamp was the fact that I had to tell my kids about my nan. I was happy because I'd taken them to see her pretty recently and she'd done an early Christmas for them because she knew her time was coming. But I felt like I was hiding behind a mask and putting a brave face on things.

The first couple of contestants who went out were told 'no', and then it was my turn. I could see the shiny, new white seats on the side of the stage and I really wanted to be sat on one. I started to sing but it was really tough because there were several times when I felt like I might break down. I was feeling wobbly and my bottom lip was going. I kept thinking about nan and the fact my family were away on holiday without me.

That performance felt like such a blur but I remember people going crazy and Sharon got very emotional and said that she'd dreamt of having a contestant like me. She pointed to the chairs and said to me, 'Get your bottom over there missus!' The Overs were the first category to try and win their places, which meant I was the first person ever in the history of *The X Factor* to sit in one of those seats; it felt pretty amazing. I had my hands over my face and people were shouting my name but I knew I wasn't safe. There were still a lot more people who were going to perform and there certainly weren't enough seats for everyone. As much as you want your fellow contestants to do well because you've bonded with them, the last thing you want is to lose your place to one of them.

We all had to fight our corners by telling the audience why we should be saved. I remember another girl called Katie Markham getting a seat, but because we'd both sung 'Clown' we kind of knew that one of us would be leaving because we were being compared a lot. When she was told she was going home she was sobbing her heart out and I felt awful. She was a lovely girl.

Eventually there ended up being just six of us on the seats and when I realised I was one of Sharon's final line-up I couldn't believe it. She came running onto the stage – we were through to Judges' Houses! It was absolutely brilliant. The first thing I thought was 'Where does Sharon live?' and it hit me that we might be going to LA!

When I got back to my hotel room and charged up my phone there was a message from Craig telling me that my nan had passed away the day before. No one had wanted to tell me until after I'd finished my audition. I was expecting it but I was devastated. She was like the unofficial head of our family and I knew she would be very much missed. I totally understand the family's decision not to tell me, especially in light of the fact that no one else involved in the competition knew about it. They had to do what they thought was right. My mum's mum Rita is the only grandparent I've got left. She's 83 and she's in a home now but she's still got all her faculties.

Now we were through to Judges' Houses things started to get more serious. We were assigned solicitors and given contracts to read through. And I had to speak to my work about taking more time off. I couldn't keep asking for weeks off here and there, so I went to see my boss and we decided a three-month career break would be best. It meant that I wasn't being paid for that time, so it was a massive risk.

I was totally skint but I needed clothes for LA if that's where we were going, because I had nothing suitable for somewhere so hot. All of the other contestants were looking more and more glamorous and I felt pretty out of my depth. Was I really capable of making it to the live shows?

CHAPTER 10

WHEN YOU BELIEVE

Craig and I had so much to sort out before I went away. We only had a couple of weeks to get organised and get visas for me, and it was still the kids' summer holidays. Our family and friends were amazing and they really helped us out, but I was panicking about missing Craig, Brooke and Tommy.

It was supposed to be top secret where we were flying out to but we'd all kind of worked it out. Plus there were loads of websites reporting that we were going to LA, so I had a pretty good idea that my initial instincts had been right. We all met up at the airport – Lorna, Shelley, Joe, Zoe, Andrea and myself – and we got handed a gold envelope which had the name of the place we were flying to inside. When we opened it up it said 'Los Angeles'. What a brilliant feeling.

The flight seemed to take forever but when we finally

touched own in LA it was amazing. We were put up in a hotel on the Sunset Strip and got to work pretty much straight away rehearsing our song choices. We did some filming driving around Venice Beach in some open-top cars, and even though I was tired because we were so busy I was also completely hyperactive. I think the adrenalin kept me going. I remember not eating very much because I was filling myself up on milkshakes instead. I think the sugar probably helped to keep me buzzing.

The following day we all had afternoon tea in Sharon's dining room at her incredible house. Caroline Flack and Matt Richardson were filming *Xtra Factor* and I got the chance to lie in the Osbourne's garden and sunbathe. I'd taken Sharon's autobiography for the journey and it was quite surreal reading it in her *actual* house. There was loads of chatter about who was going to be the guest mentor helping Sharon to decide on her final three. The crew rounded us up and Sharon walked over to us – we knew we were about to find out. 'This is *the* most incredible performer and writer and you've got to deliver the best performance of your life. Are you ready?' Sharon said. We all shouted 'yes' and then she told us to turn around on the count of three. I couldn't wait to see who it was, and when I swung round and saw Robbie Williams you could have knocked me down with a feather. I'd always had a massive crush on him and now here he was standing in front of me. Only this time I hadn't just collapsed at one of his concerts and been given a toy dummy

I met Craig in 2002. Here we are looking happy and relaxed on holiday in Turkey.

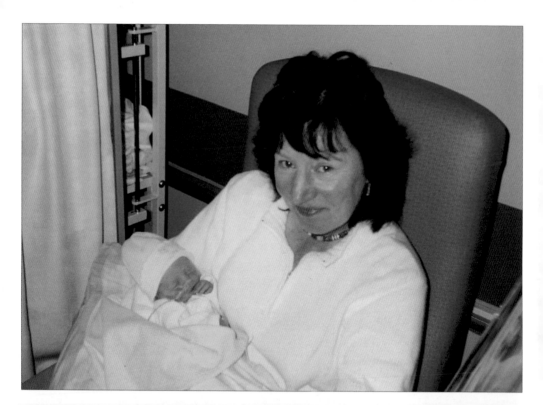

Above: My mum holding Brooke, looking very happy! I can't believe what a tiny little thing she was.

Below: Brooke with her daddy. He was in love from the second he saw her.

Brooke and Tommy have always been close. Brooke loves looking after her little brother, and now Miley too.

Above: Brooke and Tommy having lots of fun in the park.

Below: Brooke and Tommy meet Father Christmas. Tommy looks full of Christmas cheer!

Craig and I when I auditioned for *The X Factor* in 2007. I was terrified.

Above: My second audition for the 2013 edition of *The X Factor*…

Below: …and just a few months later I'm duetting with Nicole Scherzinger!

(*Above*) The moment of truth. I was genuinely shocked to win. (*Inset*) Celebrating with my mentor Sharon Osbourne. I was as happy for her as I was for me.

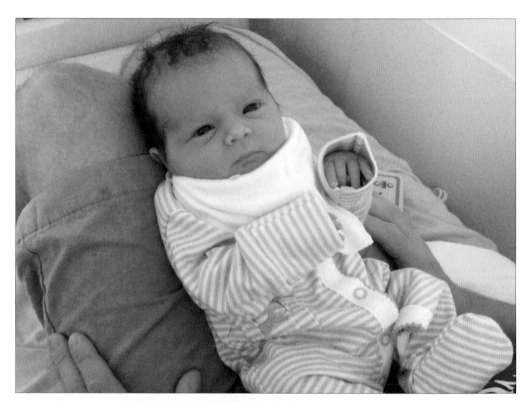

Above: My lovely Miley was born at 10:41am on the 10th September 2014.

Below: Brooke and Tommy are absolutely thrilled about having a new baby sister.

– he was going to be judging my voice and, to a certain extent, determining my future. It was like I'd come full circle from being that star-struck teenager. Now I was a star-struck 36-year-old!

Robbie asked if we were ready to perform for him, and then he walked down and said hello and gave us all a hug. He was so nice and down to earth. He told us that if we didn't 'bring the goods' he was going to chuck us in the swimming pool. I was so hot and bothered it probably would have done me some good.

Soon enough I found myself standing in front of Robbie and Mrs O and was about to start singing. I was really nervous because I wasn't sure about my song choice, 'I Have Nothing' by Whitney Houston; I was worried it might seem a bit old-fashioned. I was thinking about Craig while I was singing it, but as I walked away I started crying because I really thought I'd really messed it up. As I found out later, Robbie kind of thought the same. He said to Sharon that he wasn't sure where I'd fit in. Thank god I didn't know that at the time. I would have been in such a state.

The next day, after one of the worst night's sleep of my life, we all went back to Mrs O's to hear the verdict. We had to wait in her dining room and then when it was our turn to go and see Sharon we had to walk to the top of the house to this veranda that had a little waterfall on it. Finally it was my turn to go and find out if I'd made it through to the live finals. I wanted to do it for my family so badly. I couldn't bear the thought of having to go back and tell them I hadn't made it.

Sharon asked how I thought I'd done the previous day and I was honest and said that I didn't think it had gone brilliantly. She agreed and said that instead of moving forwards in a natural progression I'd gone backwards and she hadn't seen my usual feistiness. I burst into tears. I was certain it was all over for me and I couldn't stop crying. I was waiting for her to tell me I was going to home but then she said, 'You're going to stick with me and if you don't win this contest I'm going to kick your arse!' Oh my god!

We had a massive hug and then I ran off to see Dermot. I just remember saying, 'I want to celebrate with a cup of tea!' and that's exactly what I did. I had a nice brew and I relaxed and took it all in. Lorna came and sat with me in the garden and told me she'd got through, and I really was expecting Joe to be the third person to get onto the live shows. He was a real heartthrob and had a great voice, and he was singing for his little boy. When Shelley walked round the corner I was genuinely shocked. Not because I didn't think she was good, because I really did, but because we've got quite similar singing styles. In fact, Lorna, Shelley and I were all quite similar. It was going to be an interesting time.

We didn't get to see the contestants who didn't make it through – Zoe, Joe or Andrea – that day because they'd been taken straight down to the beach to do some filming. I was desperate to give them all a hug. Lorna and Shelley wanted to go out and celebrate but I just wanted to go back to my hotel room and have some quiet time. It had been an incredible but stressful day. Needless to say, all I wanted to do was phone my family and tell them I was through to the Lives, but it all had to be kept top secret until we got back home. The researchers stayed in touch with all of our families and let them know we were okay, but we had to save the news for the 'big reveal'.

It was soon time to head back to the UK and once we landed I was driven home where I knew everyone was waiting for me, desperate to hear the outcome. My living room was packed with about 25 of my friends and family (and, of course, a film crew). When I walked in everyone was staring at me expectantly and I couldn't even smile in case I gave the game away. My kids wanted to give me a cuddle, but they had to be really good and sit patiently until I'd broken the news. I started off by telling them what Robbie had said and admitted I thought I'd ballsed it up. Then I paused and said, 'But I'm through to the live shows!' The whole place erupted. Everyone went absolutely crazy.

My life changed beyond all recognition from that day on. Digital Spy had managed to get hold of a list of the final 12 and people were talking about me a lot online. I found myself obsessively reading things, and it was so weird that people knew who I was and were taking the time to write all of these things about me. Groups of *X Factor* fans were having full-on discussions and thankfully most of it was nice. I hadn't been seen on TV yet, so I hadn't started to be recognised in the street or anything, but things definitely felt different to how they had done a month earlier. I had a few weeks before I went into *The X Factor* house. Craig was amazing and told me he had everything covered, so I didn't have to worry about the kids, but we both knew it wasn't going to be easy.

By now I'd started to lose weight, so I had to go and buy more clothes to take into the house with me. I know people talked a lot about my weight when I was on the show, but the producers didn't put me on any kind of ridiculous diet or force me to go to the gym every day as some people reported. In the weeks running up to leaving the kids and Craig, the stress of everything definitely affected me. I was running around loads and forgetting to eat, which meant the weight was coming off.

I'd also started doing Tabata when I got through my first *X Factor* audition. I knew I wanted to get some weight off and my local gym recommended Tabata because it was something I could do at home. Tabata is basically interval training, where you work really intensely for five-minute periods at a time. You can do it in front of *EastEnders*, so it's really easy to fit into your life no matter how busy you are. I don't want people to think I was going crazy and doing it every night, because I wasn't, but it did really help. Just before I went into the house Craig and I also did MFT, which is military fitness training. That *really* makes you work. You're lifting logs and running around in mud, so you have to push yourself.

The other really important thing was that when I was working in the prison service I was eating the wrong things at the wrong times, but in the *X Factor* house I was eating three square meals a day. We had breakfast laid on and then a chef would cook us lunch and dinner, so I wasn't going to the local takeaway at 10pm to get saveloy and chips. I lost about three stone from my first audition to the final, and went from a size 18 to a 10–12.

In early October 2013 Lorna, Shelley and I were all filmed going into the *X Factor* house together in north London. It didn't seem real, this unbelievable place with a swimming pool and a massive back garden. The kitchen alone was bigger than my entire house. Someone told me it used to belong to Lionel Richie but I'm not sure if there's any truth in that. We were running around finding all of these ridiculous new rooms and I nearly fell over when I saw the music room!

Somehow – and I never, ever questioned why – I managed to get a bedroom all to myself. Everyone else had to share, but for whatever reason they put me on my own. Other people in there had kids too, but maybe it was because I was the oldest and I was married so they wanted me to have some privacy to talk to Craig?

We were kept stupidly busy and the first week was spent routine-ing our songs and practising our ensemble track, Daft Punk's 'Get Lucky'. Annie Williams, the vocal coach, went through all of our songs with us, as she did every week. We also had to have a makeover and do a photoshoot for the opening credits. I went into hair, make-up and costume wearing a dodgy leopard print top with strangely curly hair and no make-up and I came out looking completely different. They said it was the best makeover on the show – probably because I no longer looked like myself!

I was happy for them to do pretty much anything to me. I was well up for experimenting. I wasn't like, say, Tamera who had her own style. I didn't really have a style of my own, other than rather scruffy. The only thing I didn't want to do every week was wear dresses because that made me look and feel like an Over, and as far as I was concerned I was only in my mid-30s. I didn't want to look like a frumpy mum.

The first week had a 1980s theme and when we drove into Fountain Studios for the first time I'd never seen anything like it. There were so many girls and most of them were screaming for Sam Callahan. It was crazy to think that all of those people were there just for us: the final 12 acts in the competition.

The first live show itself was the most unbelievable experience, but to a certain extent I was just happy to get through it. I performed Jennifer Rush's 'The Power of Love' and the producers stuck me on a podium that had dry ice swirling around the bottom of it. I was wearing heels, which we already know aren't my forte, and just after the second verse I was supposed to walk down three stairs onto the stage. Eek. I was fine in rehearsals, but the big studio doors had been open, so the dry ice had been seeping out. But that night there was nowhere for it to escape to, so it was really thick and up to my waist. I couldn't see the steps but I had to walk forward without looking down and somehow navigate my way onto the main stage in a dress and killer heels. I was absolutely petrified. I let out a massive sigh of relief when I made it down there safely, and from that moment on I put everything I could into the song.

The standing ovation and the feedback I got from the judges made the past 20 years of hard graft feel so worth it. The only problem was that people were going so mad about my performance that I started to worry I'd set the bar too high and it was all going to be downhill from there. When I watched my performance later, all I could focus on was that my fingernails looked really stumpy because I'd bitten them down to the quick and had to have false ones put on. I should have been evaluating my singing, but instead I was thinking, 'I hope my nails have grown a bit by next Saturday'.

The kids, Craig and my mum came to see that first show and it was so lovely, but because Tommy was under six he was only allowed to watch me perform and then he had to leave the studio. My mum stayed with him but unfortunately they didn't get to see the show as the only room available for them to wait didn't have a TV!

It was also hard having to say goodbye so quickly because I missed them like mad. That became the routine: me saying goodbye to them every week and then getting really upset knowing it would be another week before I could hug them. But I'd known the deal when I auditioned for the show and it was my choice to be there, so I didn't expect sympathy. It was all incredibly tough on Craig too. He was in charge of divvying up my eight tickets each week and he got so much hassle from people because, not surprisingly, everyone wanted to come along. He was contemplating pulling names out of a hat at one point just to keep people off his back.

All of the *X Factor* contestants had been written about in the press from day one, but after that first live show things really stepped up a gear. There wasn't a day that went by when there weren't pap pictures or a story of some kind in the tabloids and online. Most of the time I let it go over my head but there were a few things printed that upset me. There was also a lot of speculation about other work I'd done. It came out that I'd auditioned for *The X Factor* previously, as I've mentioned, and I was linked to Max Clifford, but that story is nothing like it was made out to be.

In 2011 I'd been asked to do a gig in a pub called The Horse and Hound in Broadway in Worcestershire through a friend of mine called Mark Bolton, who is also a singer. My first night happened to be the same evening they were switching on their Christmas lights and loads of people were dressed in old-fashioned clothes. There was mulled wine and mince pies and the atmosphere was amazing. As I've said before, when the crowd are good, *you're* good. I was singing 'And I'm Telling You I'm Not Going' from the musical *Dreamgirls*, which was always my last song of the night, when I saw this lady walk in and walk back out again.

A few minutes later she came back in with a white-haired man who I recognised as Max Clifford.

Max came up to be when I'd finished and asked if I had a business card, which I didn't. Instead I got a beer mat, of all things, and wrote my number down for him. I didn't hear from him for a few months but then his PA contacted me and said Max had a few corporate events coming up he'd like me to perform at, and he also wanted me to sing at his upcoming birthday party that weekend. I travelled to New Malden in Surrey and went along to a beautiful Italian restaurant called Il Camino. It was a tiny little place full of all his friends. There were no celebrities at all and it was nothing like I expected. I know all sorts of things have gone on with Max recently, but I saw him as a really genuine bloke and he used to rave about me to people when no one else believed in me.

About eight months later Max asked me to perform at a charity event that was helping to raise money for British flood victims. As a result of those gigs there was all of this ridiculous stuff in the papers claiming that he'd called up Simon Cowell and told him all about me and that he had to get me to win *The X Factor*. But it's a public vote, so it's a ridiculous thing to claim! I didn't even tell Max when I went in for *The X Factor* because we hadn't spoken for ages. In fact, the first time I'd seen him since that charity concert was at the final of *The X Factor* because he was backstage.

I wasn't used to being talked about and every time something else came out in the press I'd think 'Here we go again'. I tried not to give it too much thought because it could easily have distracted me and taken my focus away from my performance each week, which was the whole reason I was in the show. I kept setting myself goals throughout the live shows and at some point the nerves started to dissipate. I got more used to standing up on stage in front of a crowd of thousands. It was like I could block them out and concentrate on singing.

But another thing that hacked me off was when someone sold a story to the papers saying that I wasn't just a prison officer, I'd also worked professionally with Beverley Knight and Lulu. I was accused of being a backing vocalist for loads of artists and people thought I was trying to pull the wool over the public's eyes. But I was doing nothing of the sort. I've mentioned before that I performed on the same bill as them at a charity concert, but I had to do a bit of damage control because that backfired on me and people thought I was being dishonest. I did work with some famous singers in the sense that we shared a stage for a night, but I wasn't on the stage at the same time as them or sharing a dressing room! I would happily be a backing singer for any of those people, so I should take it as a massive compliment, but I hated people thinking I wasn't being completely honest.

One of the most exciting things about being on the *The X Factor* was some of the amazing people we all got to meet, although I made a complete douche out of myself in front of Robin Thicke. I saw him walking down the corridor and I gasped and said to him, 'I'm not allowed to talk to you otherwise I'm going to say something really stupid. Can I possibly have a photo taken with you?' What. A. Dick. I'm not very good at having my photo taken with famous people, or even talking to them, because I still get star-struck all the time now.

There were so many people who performed on the show. Katy Perry was one and she had a massive entourage so we didn't really get to speak to her. Lady Gaga was the same. She had an army of people around her and she was so tiny we couldn't even see her. It was the same with Taylor Swift. I didn't even know she was in the building because she was kept totally separate from us.

I really liked it when acts came down to see us and gave us a pep talk in the dressing room. If I go back on the show at any point I will definitely do that. My advice will be, 'Good luck, enjoy it, channel your nerves and don't worry about letting anyone else down. This is your dream so take it day by day.'

Jessie J was absolutely amazing when she came on. She came and spoke to us all, as did Harry and Niall from One Direction. The other three members of the band walked down the corridor with their heads down and didn't even make eye contact with any of us. Harry really saved me one night because I was having a massive, massive paddy over an outfit I'd been made to wear that I didn't like. Plus there had been stuff in the papers about me that day that had upset me, so I felt like I was having a bit of a meltdown. Harry saw me crying in the corridor and he pulled me into a dressing room, grabbed me by the shoulders and said, 'I think you're amazing. You're an amazing singer. My mum loves you.' I've since become friends with Harry's mum. We chat on Twitter and meet up and we get on really, really well. She's got so much to be proud of with Harry. He's one of the good ones.

Mary J. Blige came out and spoke to us; she seemed really friendly but I think it was more her entourage that wanted to move her away from us. I reckon she would have chatted if she'd had the chance. But the absolute highlight of all the acts I met was Michael Bublé. I was the only one left in the Overs and Sharon knows Michael quite well, so I got a private meeting. It was the semi-finals and he was in a Winnebago outside the studios and Sharon took me out to meet him. I chatted to him for a while and I even sat on his lap. The crew wanted to film it but they couldn't get the camera to work, so I was quite happy to sit there for a good five minutes! Later on, when the other contestants and I were waiting to go on and do the ensemble piece, he walked past, stopped and said to me, 'I've just watched your audition. Oh my god, your voice is *amazing*!' Then he took a photo with me on his phone. On *his* phone!

Robbie Williams was brilliant, as always. He apologised to me backstage for the comments he'd made in LA and said, 'I want to take back everything I said when we were at Judges' Houses. I was really worried that you were going to be played on Radio 2 loads and people wouldn't hear enough about you but I was so wrong. You've totally got my support.' He even said on the show that he was backing me to win. Olly Murs is a lovely lad, too. I think the people who have been through the same sort of process are the ones who 'get it' and always have a few words of wisdom for you. Little Mix were blinding, such top girls. I've seen them at a few things since and I can't fault them. They're always friendly and good fun.

Rebecca Ferguson was gorgeous and James Arthur was pretty cool. Having been the previous year's winner he made sure he made time to come and have a chat with us all. It was a difficult evening for him because he had to go on stage and do a big apology for some Twitter comments he'd made. But fair play to him, he did it well and he was great to all of us. Leona Lewis was really nice to hang out with and quite shy and unassuming. I sang 'Bleeding Love' with her and it made me realise what a difficult song it is to sing and how incredible her vocal range is.

JLS were among my favourites because they were such a laugh. When us finalists performed with them on the show I was wearing these sequined trousers that were black one way, but silver if you rubbed the sequins up the other way. For some stupid reason I drew a massive willy on my leg in silver sequins during the camera rehearsals. I didn't make a big deal out of it, I just waited for people to notice, and I remember Aston and some of the crew cracking up.

I was gutted I didn't get to meet The Killers when we

were in the final. We were running around so much we didn't get a chance to say hello, but we did get to watch their performance from the side of the stage and the atmosphere was so incredible.

One of the most amazing moments of my life was when I got to meet Celine Dion, who was the nicest person ever. She was really funny and lovely and I think that's why she's still going strong now. There wasn't a hint of diva about her. I noticed that her entourage and her husband Rene sat in the canteen with everyone else. They weren't hidden away and they were friendly to everyone.

She's one of my singing idols and of course I'd been to see her at Caesars Palace in Vegas. The autograph Craig bought me had hung proudly in our conservatory for years but the sun had faded the signature, so when I met her I asked her to sign it again, which she happily did. If you'd told me in Vegas all those years ago I'd have had the opportunity to ask Celine to re-sign my picture of her, I would have said you you were insane. Her best advice was to keep going and take care of my voice, and you can't say fairer than that. She's so lovely she even tweeted to say congratulations when I won. Maybe I should frame the tweet too?

While we're on the subject of legends, I also got to hang out with Elton John, who took a selfie of the two of us on his phone. I didn't manage to get a picture of my own at the time, so I'm still trying to get hold of a copy of the one he has if anyone has got it. Elton?!

Oh yes, and let's not forget me meeting Michael Bolton… That was so unexpected, which made it even more special. We were back at the house and we were all told we had to do press interviews. Mine wasn't scheduled until 5pm and I was gutted. I knew that if I could swap with one of the others and do my interview early I could go home and see my kids, but the crew were insisting that I stick to my original time. I'm not going to lie, I was very overtired and very angry, so I went to my room and had a good old cry. I phoned Craig and I wasn't in the best mood so we ended up having a massive barney. It was such a frustrating situation and seemed really unfair.

I would say that the hardest thing about being in the show was not being able to see my family as and when I wanted. We had Internet connection in the *X Factor* house but we were all sharing it and people were downloading performances and songs and all sorts, so it was so slow. I got so upset about not being able to Skype Craig and the kids one day that one of the crew members gave me the staff password so I could use theirs. I missed them all so much.

One of the researchers came up and said that Sharon was on the phone for me. We started talking about song choices and I told her how upset I was that I couldn't see the kids. She said to me, 'You're the only contestant I've got left and I want you to put some make-up on, wear something really nice, hold your head up high and go and do that interview at 5pm. Don't show any weakness to anyone in that house.

You go out there and you show me what you've got.' With her words still ringing in my ears I pulled myself together and went downstairs to rehearse the group ensemble.

The crew said they were going to do some filming so they mic'd me up. We were just getting started when a researcher came in said someone was at the door for me. I was so confused. I knew it couldn't be Craig or the kids because they were back in Leicester, and when I opened the door Michael Bolton was standing there. I could not bloody believe it. Lorna had got to sing with him when she'd performed at G-A-Y the week after she left the show, and I was gutted because he's my favourite male singer ever. I'd had the opportunity to speak to him on the phone a couple of times but meeting him was something else.

I invited him in and we started chatting. Suddenly it all clicked and I realised why everyone had been so tricky about changing my interview time. I got a text from Sharon saying, 'Did you get your present?' and I sent her a very grateful reply. Michael and I chatted for ages about music and all sorts and I learnt so much just in that short space of time. After that I couldn't stop talking about him to the rest of the contestants and I was driving everyone mad. I was being so annoying with my Bolton babbling that one of the crew wrote 'Mrs Bolton' on my water bottle backstage.

Ridiculously, Michael (or the 'Boltmeister' as I now call him) and I have become quite good mates now and I was talking to him in LA for about an hour the other day. We recorded a track for my album and I was supposed to do a gig with him at the Royal Albert Hall earlier this year but I wasn't well, so I was absolutely wounded that I missed it. Hopefully I'll get the chance again. That would be something else.

I've got so many nice memories from being on the show but so much of it is a blur. Honestly, it went by so quickly that sometimes it didn't feel real. Some of the smallest, silliest things are the things I remember most. Craig's Auntie Susan owns bakeries in Loughborough and she makes the most amazing cobs. She used to send a load down with Craig every week and after the show we'd all have them backstage with ham and cheese; the crew used to call them 'Sam's baps'. It became a running joke that after the show all week everyone would tuck into 'Sam's baps'. I was performing with superstars and yet it's things like that which will always stay with me. I've seen a lot of the crew on other TV shows since and they'll come over and say, 'How are you Bappage?' I made some really good mates on *The X Factor*. It's just one of the many reasons I'm so grateful to the show.

It was so nice getting to know the judges too. Obviously it's every judge for themselves because they have to look after their acts, but once Gary's last act, Rough Copy, had gone he came and chatted to me and told me how much he loved my voice. Nicole was the same. She was very professional and she was really respectful and lovely, but she kept her distance to a certain extent because she was keeping an eye on her girls. Louis was a laugh and Sharon had my back throughout everything and we've stayed really close. She has been so incredible and looked after me so well and I've asked her to be godmother to our newest addition, Miley. I also asked Nicholas McDonald to be godfather. He cried his eyes out when I messaged him, he was so overwhelmed. I know they'll both be amazing.

It goes without saying that I was given the nickname 'Screwbo' while I was on the show but it didn't bother me at all. I've been called worse names before (remember Piss Flaps?). And I totally got where the comparison came from. When the public first saw SuBo on *Britain's Got Talent* they judged her straight away, and they did exactly the same with me. I took it as a compliment because they were thinking I probably looked a bit of a state, had no talent and was a tough prison officer, so when my booming voice came out they were a little shocked.

A lot was made of the prisoners supporting me on the show, but it's hard to talk about because I still see myself very much as a professional and I didn't want to make a big thing of it. But I know that some of them were saying things to each other like, 'She nicked me years ago' or 'She put me on report.' Most of them were pretty cool about it and I think there were probably a lot of discussions back in the prison about their old jacket-wearing screw being on TV.

CHAPTER 11

THE WINNER
TAKES IT ALL

I never for a minute thought I was going to win *The X Factor*. From day one I thought it would either be Sam Callahan, Luke Friend or Nicholas McDonald. They were the ones everyone was screaming for week after week. My favourite group were Kingsland Road. I absolutely loved those boys and when they left the show in week four it left a massive hole. The whole atmosphere in the house changed overnight and I would gladly have swapped them with one of the other groups. But we'll come onto that.

I know everyone rated Tamera and she did have a great voice, but in my opinion she was too young for the show. She reminded me of myself back in the day and she needed to learn to control her voice. She's got an amazing talent and I think once she's been out there and gigged a bit she'll be incredible. She got a lot of bad press so that was tough on her. She was being lifted up one day and knocked down the next. One minute she was going to be the next Rihanna and the next she was public enemy number one. I really admire how she dealt with it all.

Abi was an amazing songwriter and so quirky, and I also loved Hannah's voice. There were so many good people in the competition. Personally, my plan was go on stage every week and get the recognition I wanted and that was enough for me. I really didn't think I would be one of the final two stood there at the end of the competition. At the most I was hoping I'd get booked to do some gigs off the back of it. Now I'm playing incredible venues and I've got my own tour coming up.

I don't want to bad mouth *The X Factor* because they were brilliant in a lot of ways, but it was very hard on all of the finalists sometimes. Towards the end of the competition I felt pretty lonely. Even though there were always loads of people around us it's not the same as having those closest to you around you all the time.

We had one member of the crew who stayed in the house with us at all times to keep an eye on us and make sure we were staying sane and happy. But I was very wary of opening up to her – I was 36, so I wanted to deal with my own stuff. If I was upset I didn't want to sit down and have a conversation with someone going through all of the psychological stuff I'd learnt on the cruise ships and as a prison officer.

When I was upset I wanted to be left alone. When people

watch the show on the telly it looks like we're having the best time in the world and it looks like non-stop fun, but there was so much going on behind the scenes. We were filming constantly for the main show and *Xtra Factor*, so we were up really early and on the go all the time learning new songs and rehearsing. We couldn't just pop outside for a walk because there were fans waiting at all times, so you had to have security escorting you everywhere. Plus you had the added pressure that you were going to be performing in front of millions of people every single week and a lot of those people would be judgmental about how you looked and sounded. It was a lot of pressure.

One of the only 'normal' things I did was go to Asda with Nicky (my fellow contestant Nicholas McDonald) quite a bit. It sounds really boring but for us that was a nice little trip and a chance for a bit of normality. There were two security guys in the house who used to take us out and to be honest they were probably the only two people I had normal, sane conversations with. I used to have a cup of tea and chat to them about grown-up stuff like our children and home lives. Some of the younger finalists didn't really have any experience of that kind of thing.

We got to go on some really fun trips so we could be filmed for different show segments. We went skating and go-karting, and also to a premiere – for *Thor*, my first one ever. All the lads got invited to an Xbox launch, but I wasn't so I kicked up a right stink. Just because I was a 36-year-old woman didn't mean I didn't like gaming. And we got a free Xbox at the end of the night. Result!

Performance-wise, the only one of mine I didn't love was Adele's 'Make You Feel My Love'. It's a beautiful song and I dedicated it to Craig, but I didn't feel it had enough gumption in it for me. I prefer to do songs where I can belt really powerful vocals. One of my favourite weeks was Big Band week because I've wanted to sing with a big band ever since I worked at Pontins. Performing 'New York, New York' with Robbie Williams' *Swing When You're Winning* band was unbelievable. I liked it when I was given staging too, because it gave the performance a different feel. Most weeks the producers put me in a dress and stood me in dry ice, and I was worried the audience would get bored of me if it seemed I was doing the same thing week after week. I wanted my performances to be about the vocals but at times I felt like there was a massive gap between the other contestants and me age-wise. I was singing the fuddy-duddy songs and they were singing upbeat chart hits. I didn't want to feel dated and dull.

The same went for my clothes. I didn't know what Spanx were until I was in that show but they became my best friends. The stylists were amazing but they loved putting me in jumpsuits and I felt big in them. I thought I still had a big waist. Also, columnist Katie Hopkins called me a 'fat mum in a jumpsuit'. On the one hand I thought it was quite funny because maybe that's what I was, but on the other it was cruel and not the most supportive thing she could have said about another woman. I got a few unkind comments from the press and when you're already feeling quite tired and emotional things get to you a bit more. To hide my embarrassment about what Katie had said I started referring to myself as a 'fat mum in a jumpsuit' and trying to laugh it off. I thought that if I made a joke out of it people wouldn't think it was such a big deal.

I didn't want to let someone as blatantly headline-grabbing as Katie upset me, but when you're left in a competition with one other female who is sixteen years old and a size eight and wearing hot pants you don't feel brilliant about yourself anyway.

The hair and make-up girls were fantastic. Because I was in dresses a lot I couldn't have funky hair, I had to have diva hair. I didn't always love it but they still did a brilliant job of making me look a lot better than I did. I picked up loads of good make-up tips and I'd love to say I walk around the house with smoky eyes and red lipstick on every day but it's simply not true!

I was very lucky in that I got really good comments from the judges. The only bad one I got was from Nicole when she said that she didn't like my performance of 'Make You Feel My Love'. She was pretty direct and told me, 'This is really hard for me because I am one of your biggest fans, that performance just left me lukewarm. I didn't love that song for her and I didn't want to hear it again. True story, sorry.' But it was totally fair enough. As I said, I didn't think it was my best week and I am always open to other people's opinions. Sometimes they're the things that can drive you the most.

Thankfully, towards the end of the competition when the house started to get less busy Craig, Brooke and Tommy were able to visit me more often. There was even the odd night when I was allowed to stay at home. That's what helped get me through: just feeling like a normal family again. The closer we got to the final the more excited I got about being back home in my bed in my house in Leicester again. Hopefully once I'd won the competition, of course...

When Luke, Nicky and I got through to the final we all sat in the car on the way to the arena looking at each other going, 'Oh my god!' We couldn't believe we'd all made it so far. Because there were only three of us left in the competition there was no point in us all staying in such a big house on our own, so we were moved to a hotel, the Hilton in Wembley. Packing our stuff up took for ever. I went into the house with two suitcases and I came out with three suitcases and five giant storage bags full of stuff. I'd bought some new clothes because I'd lost weight, I'd had stuff sent to me from clothing companies, and I'd been given outfits on the show. I was even sent a free laptop by one company. I also had things fans had given me. Really lovely presents like candles and pictures.

Luke and Nicky shared a room in the hotel and I had my own. We had bouncers outside our door at all times and I'm pretty sure they weren't there for my benefit – I suspect it was more about the lads. We were so near to the final but first I had my *X Factor* homecoming, which I was really looking forward to. Poor Craig had to organise everything for 800 people to come to the Athena, a big venue in Leicester. He put an invite out on Facebook and so many people wanted to come he had to take it off again. He only had a week to get everything sorted out and loads of people were coming back to the house afterwards too, so he had to lay on food and drink. For some reason it was all left to him and he did an amazing job.

I know some people have a bit of a pop at me and say I'm not really from Leicester, but I've lived here since 2000. My kids were born here and my husband is from here. I've adopted Leicester as my home and I love where I live. I would never go back to living in London now, and who says that just because you're not born somewhere you can't belong there? It's like saying to a Liverpool player that they're not a true Liverpool player because they were born in Manchester. I've had to defend myself a lot for calling Leicester my home-town, but to me it is.

Arriving at the Athena was amazing. The mayor was there, as well as people from the local council and radio stations. There were banners and T-shirts and people asking for autographs. There were even fireworks. I couldn't keep the smile off my face. The screaming was so loud when I walked up the red carpet I was overwhelmed. Getting that kind of support from my hometown was such a boost.

When we got inside, the kids and Craig came up on stage with me and I asked Tommy who he liked best from *The X Factor*. Thankfully he said me! I also asked Brooke and I was really worried she was going to say Luke or Nicky because I knew she was a fan of theirs. I told the crowd that the song I was going to sing was for my babies. I performed 'Clown' and I meant every single word. I was on the brink of tears and I wasn't sure I'd be able to get to the end of the track. I was so happy to see everyone. When I finished Tommy gave a little bow and it broke my heart. It helped me to remember what the last six months had been all about. It was about trying to make a better future for my family.

I got to stay at home that night and we had a nice, normal family evening watching TV and eating chocolate. The following day I got dolled up and was picked up and taken to Eyres Monsell social club, which was absolutely heaving. I chose to go there because it's got a few different rooms and the local kids love it. I've performed there before; it's a bit rough at times but very family orientated and it felt right.

I think people were a bit shocked to see Sharon Osbourne, of all people, walk in. She was hilarious as usual and went behind the bar to pull a pint. We did a duet of 'The Shoop Shoop Song (It's in His Kiss)' together on the karaoke and I couldn't have asked for a better reception. I was interested to see whether people would treat me differently back home but they didn't. I was the same old Sam. Only this time I had TV cameras and Mrs O with me.

Back in London all the preparations were being made for the grand final at Wembley Arena. We were going to be performing to the entire venue, which seated 10,000 people. Nicky, Luke and I sat backstage in the dressing room on the Saturday and there was so much going on. We were given Dressing Room One, which is a really nice one, and because it was the final people were running around getting us whatever we wanted. And what did we want? Nando's. Our dressing room was a right state by the end of the night.

Crew members were coming and going and celebs were arriving and I turned to the boys and said, 'This is all for us! This is all about us three! Do you not find that unbelievably amazing that the whole reason this night is happening and millions of people will be watching is because we're going to be performing. That's an achievement in itself and whatever happens from now on happens. Good luck to all of us.' I can honestly say that I would have been happy if either of those boys had won. Of course I was hoping I would win, but I wouldn't have begrudged either of them their victory, and I was still retaining a healthy scepticism in case things didn't work out.

We all had our winner's songs ready to go, having recorded them a few weeks before and I was really happy with mine. I was originally supposed to record a track called 'A Thousand Years' by Christina Perri but it was changed to Demi Lovato's 'Skyscraper' while we were in the studio, and I think that song suited my voice much more.

When we were filming during rehearsals, the producers flashed something up on the big screen and told us all to watch. That was the moment we found out that the winner would get the chance to support Beyoncé on one of her UK dates. I refused to build my hopes up because I didn't want to get excited about something that wasn't yet real. I couldn't fathom it.

A lot of the other contestants were coming back to perform Katy Perry's 'Roar' together at the Sunday night final, so they were also there at rehearsals, which was a good laugh. It kind of eased the tension having other people there to mess around and chat with.

On the first night of the final I sang Lady Gaga's 'Edge of Glory' as well as 'And I Am Telling You I'm Not Going' from *Dreamgirls*, which was a duet with Nicole. The press said that Nicole sang way more than me and that she oversang, but if anything it was really only the last note. I was supposed to come in after her but she held onto the note for so long I didn't get the chance. I told her to let the Holy Spirit take over as we went on and I guess it did – and then some! Everyone was saying she totally overpowered it and stole my thunder, but I don't think that was the case. I loved singing with her.

I was really gutted when Luke was sent home that night, but at the same time I was happy for Nicky because we were so close and I knew we'd have a great time together on the Sunday. I'd watched Luke's popularity grow massively during the show, so I knew he would be okay and do brilliant things whatever happened.

Nicky and I were back at Wembley bright and early the next day. It was going to be a *long* one, so we stole as many quiet moments as we could during rehearsals. There were ridiculously good performers on that night. Gary Barlow was duetting with Elton John. Nicky and I felt a bit bad because Elton had been given the dressing room we'd made such a mess of the day before. Mind you, it didn't *look* a mess by the time he arrived at the studios. He invited Nicky and I to go and have a chat with him and it was a totally different room. It was unbelievable: velvet drapes, a plush carpet, sofas and a champagne fridge, a million miles away from the Nando's filled state it had been the previous night.

Loads of my friends and family came along to support me, including my nan Rita. We lost her at one point when she went to the toilet and it turned out she'd been mobbed by people asking for photos. I think she secretly loved it.

The day passed in a flash and before I knew it the show had started and it was time for the group song. Everyone on that show had worked so hard and doing that would be acting like we thought we were better than them. I messed up the group song a bit. I started in the wrong key, which made Nicky go wrong. Thankfully he handled it really well and instead of being cross he looked at me and we both laughed. It wasn't the ideal start but the only way was up!

That night I sang 'The Power of Love' and 'Skyscraper'. Both songs went really well, but I've watched the final back a couple of times and I see so many little things I'd like to change. I'm so hard on myself. I just see myself sweating and my make-up running! I got great feedback but there was no telling who was going to be crowned *X Factor* winner.

When it was time for the results to be announced Sharon came on stage and stood next to me and I think we were both in a state of shock. We were waiting for Dermot to read out the all-important name but he was taking *forever*. All I could hear was the audience screaming and the sound of a very loud, thumping heartbeat.

The press had been saying for a couple of weeks that I'd won it because of the voting figures, but it was far from a done deal. I was worried that if people thought I was a sure thing they wouldn't bother to pick up the phone to vote for me, and instead they'd cast their vote for the person they saw as the underdog – Nicky.

It felt like Dermot waited hours before he said my name, but when he did there was a slight pause before it sunk in. I turned around and Sharon was on her knees in tears in complete disbelief. I looked at her and I was so happy because she'd succeeded in what she wanted to do: she wasn't ever going back to *The X Factor* and she wanted to go out with a bang. And she really had.

It was a real 'pinch me' moment for me, too. I knew that my life would never be the same again. Nicky came over and gave me a big hug and when I looked down Gary and Nicole were cheering. Sharon and I had a massive hug and she was laughing her head off. Dermot told me I got over a million votes and I was in such a state of shock I could barely speak. I remember saying that I loved Nicky McDonald to death and that he had to get an album out. I was crying and when Nicky said if he could lose to anyone it would be me, I was in bits.

Sharon was so happy. In fact, she bought me a Louis Vuitton suitcase to say thanks! I was so excited to have a real Louis Vuitton, one that wasn't from Turkey. Sharon is so pukka. Out of anyone she could easily play the big 'I am' but she's so down to earth. I've never met anyone else like her and I'm not sure I ever will.

As soon as I left the stage I was whisked off to do interviews and Craig was left stranded. He was absolutely livid because he hadn't had a chance to see me and he was almost in tears. When we did finally get to see each other *The X Factor* wanted to film our 'emotional reunion' so we couldn't really relax properly. The whole night was phenomenal but I did miss sharing it with Craig and the kids.

There was an aftershow party backstage and when I walked in hundreds of people were staring at me. A VIP area had been roped off for me and there was a bright red sofa with 'X Factor Winner' written on it. I was so embarrassed I made everyone else come and sit with me. There was champagne laid on but I was more interested in the cake section. Instead of celebrating with booze, I ate coconut macaroons and drank tea. I had my photos taken with tons of people and signed a lot of autographs but I called it a night pretty early because I had to get up and appear on GMTV and *This Morning* the following day.

I stayed in the Corinthia Hotel in Westminster that night to be close to the ITV studios, and it was beautiful. My room had a TV in the bathroom and I was so impressed, but all I wanted was for Craig, Brooke and Tommy to be there. I think it was harder knowing that I could have seen them down at the show but there hadn't been much time. Craig had driven back to Leicester because the kids had school the next day and he was really angry they hadn't got to see me properly. I phoned him and I kept saying to him, 'It's only a week and then I'll be home. Just hang in there.'

I did a lot of TV shows, interviews and signings the week after the final and it was knackering but it's part of winning *The X Factor*. What was really weird was how many people were running around after me. It was like I had a proper entourage, but I felt really uncomfortable with it. I had people dressing me and offering to get me food or drinks, and it's just not me. If someone offered to make me a cup of tea I'd say no and then go and make myself one a while later. I remember at one point I said I really liked this pair of Nike Air Max trainers and the stylist went out and got me two pairs. It was insane.

Craig was still holding the fort at home and I couldn't

wait to get back to him. The only time the kids were seeing me was on TV, but thankfully I got to go home for one night midweek because Leicester City invited me along to sing during a match at half time. I was like an excited kid. I was out in the middle of the field for a game against Manchester City and as a long-term supporter you can't get much better than that.

Finding out that my single had got to number one was incredible too. I went to Radio One to do an interview and they broke the news to me. My record company Sony gave me a massive bunch of flowers and I got an award from the Official Charts Company.

More recently I was given an award from the prison service as part of the prison officer of the year awards, which means the world to me. It was a statue of a prison door and underneath there was an inscription that read, 'In recognition of Sam Bailey, winner of *The X Factor* 2013, for raising public awareness of the positive work performed by the Her Majesty's Prison Service in protecting the public and reducing reoffending.' I was so touched.

The only fly in the ointment of winning *The X Factor* was something that I found out afterwards. I'm not going to lie; Rough Copy were quite arrogant but I put it down to them being lads. I've worked in a prison, so I've seen men with loads of bravado, but as soon as they got voted out the whole house was an easier place to be. I knew I wasn't their favourite person but I was never confrontational about it. If someone doesn't like me, fair enough, but I still have the respect and professionalism to talk to them. All in all, we didn't have the smoothest relationship and I think they had a problem with me going as far as I did in the competition. But I knew I was going to be on tour with them and I wanted things to be as easygoing as possible.

However, not in a million years did I expect one of them to do what they did later that night. I was on stage after I'd won, singing 'Skyscraper' for the second time. All of the other acts ran on cheering and I was covered in lipstick and confetti. Joey from Rough Copy stood next to me on stage, grabbed Nicky's head and mouthed, 'Nicky's the champion, Nicky's the winner', pointing to him, just inches away from me. He wasn't stabbing me in the back: he was stabbing me in the eye because he was being so blatant about it.

I didn't know anything about it until someone told me afterwards and I was mortified. I couldn't believe someone could do that. The most annoying thing is that that piece of footage became part of the video for 'Skyscraper', so people can blatantly see it. I've seen Joey since and I haven't mentioned anything, and I've had a laugh and a joke with the band, and I am working on forgiving him. I don't like to bear a grudge but it's something that I won't forget.

Meanwhile, back home things had been tough on Craig, and it wasn't until I got home myself that I realised just how tough. It had been so much harder for him than he was letting on. He didn't want to tell me when I was in the competition in case it made things more difficult for me and so he kept quiet. All he saw was me looking like I was having a really glamorous experience, and even though I told him how much hard work it was at times, it was hard for him to get his head around.

I definitely had a few meltdowns during my time in the show but Craig was the one who was really being put through it behind the scenes. Our friends and family pulled together and helped as much as possible but he was exhausted, bless him. He says he's now got the utmost respect for single working parents because he had four or five months of being on the go from 6am until 10pm, taking the kids to school, then working *and* having to do the washing, ironing and cooking.

The show definitely did put pressure on our relationship at times, but it wasn't anything major. Some of the press really went to town and made out we were on the brink of splitting up but it was never that bad. We had the odd argument but what couple wouldn't if they were under that kind of strain? And things are so much better since. Having that time apart made us appreciate each other more than ever. We had become so busy that we'd almost forgotten how to have fun. We were constantly working and when one was coming in the other was going out and we'd stopped going on 'dates' and enjoying each other's company. We do more things together now and I think the show taught us to appreciate each other more. We've just celebrated our tenth wedding anniversary and we're in a better place than ever.

We all had a brilliant family Christmas in 2013 and I think it meant even more because we'd been apart for so long. I hadn't done any Christmas shopping because I was so busy that Craig had to do it all, but he did a really good job. However, as soon as my money came through for winning of course I got overexcited and went out and got more stuff. I couldn't help myself. We didn't spoil the kids too much – well, no more than usual – but there were certain things that I wanted to get them, like a Wii U.

Craig and I went to Asda to do the food shopping on Christmas Eve and instead of the usual half an hour it took us over two hours. Every time I went up a different aisle I had a queue of people asking for autographs and photos. In the end Craig had to leave me and go and do the shop on his own because we would have been there all night.

I also got to spoil the people who helped Craig and I out so much when I was away, like Greg and Laura and Gavin and Sarah (Craig's brothers and their other halves). I got the lads an Xbox One each and I took the girls to Beaverbrooks to buy them a Michael Kors watch each, and then I treated them to dinner in an Italian restaurant called San Carlo in Leicester. I got tickets for Craig's mum to go and see Michael Bolton and she got to meet him afterwards, and I think it's fair to say she quite enjoyed that. But they all deserve all that and more. There's no way we could have gone through *The X Factor* without them.

Craig's firm, Vaclensa in Manchester, were amazing about everything. They were so supportive and they allowed him to take time off or move his shifts around when he needed to. They were really understanding and there aren't many jobs that would help out like they have.

The one thing I promised Brooke when I went into the show was that after it was finished I'd take her to France. She was learning loads about it at school and she was desperate to go. So on New Year's Day we went to Paris for the night and then on to Disneyland Paris. It was amazing. I said I'd take her to see the sights and I kept my promise. She got to go up the Eiffel Tower and see the Louvre. Disneyland was amazing and that was one time when I didn't mind getting special treatment! We had a guide with us at all times and we didn't have to queue for any of the rides. The kids absolutely loved it (okay, Craig and I probably did a bit too much, too).

I started recording my debut album on 18th January 2014 at Metropolis recording studios in Woking. It had a tennis court and swimming pool, so it was very luxurious and such a good experience. I love working on music and it was a dream come true for me. I was in the studio for around two weeks and funnily enough Nicky was there recording too, so we got to have a good catch-up.

I also caught up with a certain Mr Bolton. We did a duet, 'Ain't No Mountain High Enough', which you will have heard if you've got my album. Michael is such a witty, laid-back guy and he's kind of been like a guardian angel to me in some ways. We went for dinner a while ago and I had to phone Craig and say, 'If you see some pap shots of me coming out of a restaurant with Michael Bolton, it's all above board, okay?'

I performed at the National Television Awards during my first week at the studio and I felt like a proper celeb. I had my own dressing room and Michael and I opened the show with 'Ain't No Mountain High Enough'. The kids' choir from *Educating Yorkshire* did backing vocals and they were brilliant. I spent time with Michael during the day and he helped to steady my nerves because that's a massive deal for me. Also, because all of the kids in the choir were so nervous I felt like I had to step up a bit and be strong for them, which helped me to keep focused.

I also sang 'The Power of Love' during the awards and it was my first solo performance since *The X Factor*. What a crowd to do it in front of! I was like a properly excited fan because I got to meet so many TV stars. I told Danny Dyer to fuck off for a laugh, just because I could, and he was such a nice bloke. I saw Shane Ritchie again, the cast of *Mrs Brown's Boys* and Hayley from *Corrie*. I was in showbiz heaven.

In another case of *amazing* timing by me, when I got back from recording the album I discovered I was expecting baby number three. I had sore boobs – which, as I've said, is always the giveaway for me – so I took a test (in Asda of all places!) and when it showed up as positive I burst into tears because I felt like I'd let everyone down. I was mortified. I was bawling my eyes out. As well as thinking I'd been a total idiot I was also scared of going through childbirth again and having all the pain.

I really wanted another baby before I entered for *The X Factor*, but Craig and I didn't have the money or the space at the time. I always saw myself having three children but we were realistic about the fact I'd have to take time off work and we'd have to get an extension on the house. We didn't want the kids to have a share a room because we had a new baby. It wasn't fair. A lot of people get pregnant and then worry about things afterwards but we didn't want to do that. We were probably almost *too* sensible about it all.

Craig and I did finally manage to laugh about it when we were going round the aisles. We both looked at each other and suddenly cracked up. I think that was the moment I properly thought about how incredible it was going to be having another child rather than worrying about what people would say about it.

The baby had been conceived on New Year's Eve before I performed at a club called G-A-Y. Craig and I were staying in a hotel around the corner and we had a spare five minutes! That's what happens when you take a woman away from her husband for four months. I was so scared about telling my management company; I thought they'd be furious, but they were brilliant and said it was great news. I know some people have said I've been stupid to get pregnant and that it will ruin my career but I'm beyond happy to have three kids. If anything it will make me work harder because I want the best for all of my children. They will always come first in everything.

I was able to work throughout quite a bit of my pregnancy. I just had to take things easy when I needed to. I had to move my tour from October to January 2015, and I had to turn down a lot of things abroad because I couldn't fly. But apart from that I carried on as normal. I did a lot of gigs and festivals, so the new arrival was well-travelled before she even came into the world. I was due to do a charity event when I was seven months pregnant called 'An Evening with Sam Bailey' and I really thought I was going to have to pull out because I was feeling pretty terrible. Thankfully, in the end I managed to get there okay. I kept thinking how awful it would have been if they'd had to change the title of the night to just 'An Evening...'

I started rehearsals for *The X Factor* tour soon after I found out I was pregnant and of course because it was such early days I wanted to keep it a secret for as long as possible. But that didn't prove easy. On the first day Sam and Luke came running up to me and got me in a headlock and I was like 'Uh-oh, I'm going to have to say something'. I didn't want to tell Sam because he was going out with Tamera, so of course he would want to tell her. Tamera would then have told Hannah, and Hannah would have told Rough Copy and... You get the picture. So instead I pulled Nicky and

Luke to one side and told them, but I swore them to secrecy. They were so excited for me, bless them. I also had to tell the two choreographers because I had to be careful with the dance moves. I didn't want the dancers to think I was being a diva if I wasn't joining in but of course there were certain things I couldn't do.

In the end it all got a bit too much for me keeping the news from everyone, so when we had our end-of-tour meeting I announced it to the other acts. I think people thought I was going to do some kind of inspirational speech but instead I announced that I was having a baby. Ironically, Rough Copy were really sweet about it and hilariously kept asking people around the table if they were the father. Everyone congratulated me and they were genuinely happy for me.

My kids were very funny when we broke the news to them. We bought them both an iPad Mini each and sat them down in our living room. When I said, 'Mummy and daddy are having another baby', Brooke just said, '*Really?*' and all Tommy cared about was what mummy was hiding behind her back. They told everyone at school the next day and they were genuinely over the moon.

It wasn't long until the news leaked out to the papers but because of the laws regarding the press they weren't allowed to announce it until I was 12 weeks gone unless I gave them permission, which in the end I did. People were already talking about it and I thought there was a good chance it could come out on the Internet. If it was going to come out,

I wanted it to come from me. I also put a post on Twitter with a picture of my ultrasound of Peanut, as we'd started calling my bump, on Twitter. I got a few unkind comments but overall people were incredibly positive and supportive.

As well as things getting back on track with Craig and I, being on the show really helped to bring other members of my family back together because to a certain extent things had become a bit fragmented. I'd had to disown Danny for a while because he had followed my parents down the drinking route and he was turning into a total nightmare. I'd tried to help him several times and when I couldn't I had to leave him to help himself. I told him he couldn't contact me and he couldn't see my kids. It was a classic case of tough love.

I had to do that three times in order to try and make him change, but he's doing really well now. He's working for the mental health charity Mind, he's got his own little flat and he's changed so much. He still drives me up the wall like all brothers do, but it's so nice to see him back on his feet. Now his passion is helping other people. I don't think he'll ever go back to being the person he was before because that person lost him a lot of friends and family.

Danny is back in touch with his son Jason again now. They didn't see each other for some time when his drinking was bad, but they've got a good, solid father and son relationship. Jason looks the spitting image of Danny. Jason is a lovely lad. We had some making up to do but it's all going really well. He's got a little girl of his own now called Amelia, so our family is growing.

Charlie was also a drinker for a while but now he's met someone and he's settling down. I guess it takes some people longer than others to get themselves together. My brothers were never going to be stockbrokers and wear sharp suits but as long as they're doing what they want to do, that's okay with me. I always had this dream growing up of being able to go to my big brothers and borrow money off them and hang out at their big houses, but I wouldn't swap them for anything.

I would never want to turn around and give them money or act flash, and actually they've never asked me for anything. I like to think if they were ever really struggling they would come to me, and I have helped other people out in the past, but I also don't want to seem like the easy option. I love treating people but there's a fine line between helping people and hindering them by not letting them stand on their own two feet.

Your family is what moulds you and I did learn from them, especially when it came to things I *didn't* want to do. I've seen the negative effects of drink and drugs up close and I never wanted to go back down that black hole. Sadly, when I go back to where I grew up some people are still doing the same things. They still go to the same pubs and have the same conversations and they're stuck in negative patterns.

I've told my daughter how my dad died. She knows it

was to do with alcohol and she's funny because if we have a party I'll see her watching Craig and she'll say to him, 'How many drinks have you had?' I don't want her to be scared of alcohol but I want her to be aware of the dangers of it, and then it's up to her to make a choice about whether or not she wants to drink when she's older.

Brooke is also very aware of my mum's drinking when she comes to stay. She'll say to me, 'Is Nanny Jac drinking loads today?' because she doesn't like it when she gets a bit rowdy. I always wind Mum up when she starts getting wobbly by asking her if she's drinking enough water. She still likes a drink or eight and, much like back in the days when her and dad rowed, sometimes she tips over the edge and gets a bit nasty. I always say there are three phases to her drinking. In phase one she's happy-go-lucky and friendly to everyone. In phase two she starts dancing like nobody's business and being really talkative. In phase three she starts getting really opinionated and says stuff she doesn't really mean; everything she's thought but hasn't been brave enough to say comes tumbling out.

When Mum gets to the second half of phase three she can say some pretty awful things if the mood takes her. She also gets really defensive but we all find it funny. We don't take it seriously at all because we know what to expect and she doesn't mean anything by it. She just lets everything come tumbling out after a few too many. One of her favourite phrases is: 'I know you all hate me and wish I wasn't here.'

She'll start crying about all sorts of things you didn't even know she was upset about. You don't even want to be in the same room as her when she's like that. She gets so out of control and one time she tripped over our dog, Molly, and smashed her face. Brooke was so upset because she looked terrible, but Mum just shrugged it off.

Just like in the old days, Mum won't remember a thing in the morning. She'll get up and say, 'Do you fancy a cup of tea?' and I'll be like, 'Do you now realise what you were like last night?' I can handle it these days because I can make a joke of it and remind her about all of the things she said the night before. I can have a bit of a laugh with her, whereas back when I was a kid there was nothing funny about the drinking situation. But it's all been a big learning curve.

I would hate for anyone to think badly of my mum because she's a wonderful person and I think the absolute world of her. She's supported me and been my rock all of my life, and she still is to this day. There's nothing she won't do for me. I have so much respect for her because she hasn't always had the easiest time of it but she's come out smiling. I'm so grateful she's my mum and if there's one thing I want to say to her it's 'thank you'. She's taught me so much and been there for me throughout everything.

CHAPTER 12

GREATEST LOVE
OF ALL

In February I headed out on the *The X Factor* tour, which was the perfect opportunity to thank some of the people who had voted for me. I mainly hung around with the sound guys because a lot of the other acts and dancers were going out partying and it wasn't my scene – especially as I was pregnant.

The show started at 7.30pm every night and I was last on and I sang seven songs, so I also felt a bit separated from the others because they hung around together a lot backstage. We all did the last song together, and it was nice that we all came together, but I still felt disconnected from them. I came back home a lot to see the family, whereas most people stayed and travelled on the tour bus. If we were in a location where I could drive or fly home easily I would. It cost a small fortune but it was so worth it. The kids and Craig also got to come to a lot of the shows and bring friends, so we were all together a lot and it was a really special time.

I got pretty spoilt on the road. I had a really bad back for a lot of it, so the tour manager used to call in a masseuse for me. The catering crew were amazing, too. They used to make special meals for me and I had a secret stash of chocolate and Twister lollies to keep me going. If the kids came backstage they would make them whatever food they wanted too, so they were well happy.

I spent a lot of time with the crew and there was a guy called Gavin who organised all the meet-and-greets and was hilarious. We were always messing about and he loved a practical joke. On the rare occasions I went on the tour bus, the young acts would be up the back playing loud music and drinking. It was impossible to chill out or sleep because it was so loud. I used to sit at the front in what we called the 'sane' section, where all of the older people were, but the noise really travelled!

After one show we all went out clubbing and of course I went home early. The next day we had a really long journey on the bus and everyone was so hungover it was silent at the back. People were asleep in the gangways and all sorts. You could have heard a pin drop. Gavin decided to get his revenge for all the times the youngsters had kept us awake, so he started singing 'Little Donkey' at the top of his voice and we all joined in. The tables had well and truly turned. Then Gavin got on the microphone and started reading out

Dear Deidre from *The Sun*. It was hilarious. Although maybe not for the people who had been up until stupid o'clock the night before and had cracking headaches.

There was a bit of trouble on the tour when a couple of the other acts got into a bit of an altercation. I didn't actually see it but the story got leaked to the press, and the guy who was on the receiving end, Sam Callahan, had to wear so much make-up to cover his bruises he looked like Barbara Cartland. Poor guy. It caused a lot of tension, which was a real shame, and the guy who threw the punch quite rightly got sent home.

It was sad saying goodbye to everyone when the tour came to a close. I've seen Nicky, Luke, Kingsland Road and Rough Copy since, and it's always nice to catch up. Yes, even with Rough Copy. I've seen Shelley a bit too, and Annie, the *X Factor* vocal coach, is going to be singing backing vocals on my tour, which I'm really pleased about. I'm so excited about the tour. It's going to be me singing my heart out with an amazing band behind me and I can't wait.

I had my night opening for Beyoncé on 24th February at the LG Arena in Birmingham, but sadly I didn't get to meet her. I was kind of hidden away in a little cupboard in the lorry compartment and I was gutted. I got three minutes to sound-check and I had no lighting effects whatsoever when I performed, just one spotlight. It sounds like I'm moaning – and I kind of am, I suppose – but it would have been nice for her to say hello!

Still, the happier news is that my album went to number one for Mother's Day on 30th March 2014, which was the best feeling ever. It felt really poignant and it was a real relief because I was nervous about how it would do. I performed at G-A-Y again the night before and owner Jeremy Joseph and I had a massive cake fight on stage, which was a good way to have an early celebration! I also got a phone call from Simon Cowell congratulating me, which was surreal. I honestly thought it was Rory Bremner or someone phoning up and doing an impression of him. He was really sweet and he knew all about my kids and asked after them and how my pregnancy was going. I met him face-to-face for the first time at a charity event and he was just as nice there. He's a genuinely lovely guy.

After a year of being in the spotlight, I'm kind of used to fame now. It's weird that everyone knows who I am and people are always coming up to me to say hello when I'm shopping in the supermarket with my kids. They always say that they're surprised I'm in there doing my shopping, as if I've got a team of staff who do it all for me. I think that's hilarious. Even if I was a multi-millionaire I would still want to do all of my own everyday chores. It's what keeps me grounded.

I think people expect me to go glammed up like someone off *Dynasty*, or like I am on TV so they're a bit shocked when they see me in jeans and a T-shirt. But the whole glamour thing just isn't me. I guess in some ways I'm still the same tomboy I've always been. I want to carry on being me. I like it when I have my hair and make-up done and people think 'Wow!' but I also think it's funny when people see me in everyday life and think 'Wow, you look rough'. This is who I am. If someone wants to glam me up then great, but I've got three kids and I don't have time to do it every day.

There are certain mums on the school run that always look so well turned out and I really admire them but it must be exhausting. I've actually said to some of them, 'How the hell do you manage to look so good when you've got kids to get ready?' 'You must get up at four in the morning just to do your hair?' 'When do you get the chance to iron clothes and do the packed lunches?'

Not much has changed with my day-to-day life really. I still live in the same house I have done for the past 12 years and people are always shocked when they come round. I'm sure everyone thinks I should be living in a mansion somewhere. We're having an extension built on to our place after I finish my tour so that we've got more room for the baby, but it's my home and I love it. Maybe we'll move at some point in the future but my kids can play out the front with their friends here and they love it, so I don't want to take them too far away whatever happens.

I also still shop in the same places I always have done. I'm not swanning into Chanel and spending fortunes. I would be furious with myself if I did. I may have the odd designer piece in my wardrobe that I've been given, and I've treated myself to something from All Saints every now and again, but I'm not about to start spending £2,000 on a handbag. Why do I need something that expensive?

The kids' clothes still come from supermarkets and high-street shops too. I don't see the point in buying them really expensive clothes, because they're going to get covered in spag bol. They want to go out and play and not worry about getting messy, and at the end of the day Tommy would rather have a bright pair of Spiderman trainers than some fancy ones from Hugo Boss. The only time the children get anything slightly fancy is when we go to the outlet shopping centre in Bicester Village.

My kids are far from spoilt and I'm so lucky because they've got really kind natures. I recently did a gig for a children's charity called Destination Florida – which I'm now a patron for – and when I explained to Brooke what I was doing and told her how auctions work, she disappeared upstairs and came back down with five Loom bands for the auction. After I'd performed, I told everyone what Brooke had done and her bracelets ended up selling for £500 – that's £100 each! When I told Brooke she was so happy I thought she would burst.

When things like that happen it makes me stop and think how lucky I am that I can use my 'fame', or whatever you want to call it, for good. Let's be honest, if I'd been nobody it's likely those bracelets would not have sold at all, so to be able to raise that amount of money for the charity when doing so little meant so much.

I've got a friend called Leanne who I used to work with at HMP Gartree. She's got two lovely little kids called Mia and Corey. They've both got a very rare condition that means that they're severely disabled. She'd been trying to raise money to get her house modified for their wheelchairs but she was finding it a struggle, so when I got invited on *Tipping Point: Lucky Stars* I donated the money I won to the Strong Bones charity, which helps families like hers.

I got offered a magazine deal for my baby shower but they told me the more famous faces that were there, the more money I would get. I didn't want my friends to think they had money on their heads so I turned it down. Instead I invited along a photographer, sold the photos and gave all of the money to Leanne. If I'm ever having a bad day I think about things like that and it makes me feel so grateful. There are some incredible people in this world that do incredible things and while I may not be saving lives doing my job, at least I can give back and help as many people as I can.

I've always been realistic about the future. Craig and I have got new cars but they're both leased, so if my career kicks the pan we can give them back and we're not saddled with loads of debt. I know how this industry works and this time next year nobody might care about me. I'm not going to sit back and say, 'I've made it now,' because that's not the case. I've won a talent show but it's not the be all and end all. Yes, my life will never be the same and I'll probably get recognised for the rest of my life to a certain extent, but I still live a totally normal life – with a few crazy times thrown in here and there for good measure!

People are generally really nice wherever I go. The only place I sometimes get abuse is on Twitter because it's very easy for people to hide behind their computers. I'm lucky because I don't take offence and I actually think it's quite funny. I'm pretty tough so I can take a bit of criticism. If someone says they think I'm rubbish and they tag me in on purpose I'll either ignore them or reply with something like: 'Thanks mate! Lol!' If you stand up to a troll, they usually try and dig themselves out of the hole and apologise, but by that point I've moved on. I don't know anyone who doesn't get hassled on Twitter sometimes, even if they're not famous, and life is way too short to worry about people who haven't got anything positive to say.

I'm lucky that people are very respectful about where I live because I'm probably not that hard to track down. Very occasionally someone will come to the door asking for an autograph, and the other day four women were waiting in a car when I got home to talk to me, but generally I don't get bothered at all. What *is* weird is that people I've known for years sometimes treat me differently. Just after I'd won *The X Factor* last Christmas, I went round to Craig's cousin Lucy's house for a party and people who I'd been friends with for ages were taking photos of me and putting them on Facebook or Twitter. They were doing selfies and posting them saying: 'Look who I'm with!' but they'd known me for years! 'Skyscraper' came on TV at one point and everyone was drunk and singing along and I thought that was an ideal time to leave. When we left I said to Craig, 'I've just been treated differently', and I didn't like it very much. I want people to treat me like the same Sam they always have.

Friends and family are really good now and they know there's a time and a place for photos and autographs, and it's probably not at the dinner table at Christmas. That party felt weirder than being recognised in the street, if I'm honest.

As well as dealing with my newfound fame I was getting used to being pregnant for the third time and I kind of knew what to expect. I got a bit mardy sometimes and went into weird moods over stupid things, like Craig making something I didn't want for dinner, but I knew when I was being irrational and I'd laugh about it a few minutes later. Hormones are so ridiculous!

I was due to go into the recording studio in London back in June but I got as far as Watford when I started contracting and having pain so I had to cancel it and drive all the way back home again. I went to hospital and the doctors were so worried I was going to go into early labour they kept me in for six days in total. It turned out I had dehydration and a water infection, both of which were causing me to contract.

When I was finally let out of hospital I was given some time off to rest but I was really aware that I still had to record some songs for the Christmas reissue of my album.

My management were amazing and said they didn't want me to travel so they found a studio in Leicester and I eventually went in on 8th September. I was there all day and everyone was fussing over me and making sure I was okay. I had to stand up a lot to record the tracks and I found myself rocking from side to side a lot to try and get comfortable. I had a stool so I could sit down whenever I wanted but I was determined to get everything done and dusted that day – heavily pregnant or not.

Craig came and picked me up at 5.45pm and I remember saying to him that I had bad back ache from all of the standing up and all I wanted to do was go home, have a hot bath and go to bed. Going to sleep that night was bliss.

The following morning my midwife, Jo Proud, came round to do a check up. We were sat down chatting and she suddenly looked at me and said: 'Sam, you're contracting.' I'd been tightening for about two hours and yet somehow I still felt fine and I was able to pick the kids up from school and do everything else I had planned that day. Some of the other mums commented that I was walking a bit funnily and it's hard to explain but I felt kind of 'open' down there, like I had a cricket ball between my legs.

I phoned the hospital and said I was a bit concerned and the nurse said to me: 'You're classed as 37 weeks today which means you're full term, but you don't have to come in unless your waters have broken or you're having proper contractions. You're better off staying at home and having a bath.'

I tried my best to relax but by the evening I couldn't get comfortable on the sofa no matter how I lay so I sat on an exercise ball. I was bouncing away on it for ages and it gave me some much-needed relief. I was watching a show called *Hot Tub Britain* at the time and I was thinking 'I'd kill to get into one of those right now'.

Before Brooke when to sleep that night I said to her: 'If I go into labour tonight I need you to be a really good girl and help mummy and daddy out. I need you to help get Tommy ready for school and make the packed lunches.' I just had a feeling it was going to happen really soon.

When I went to bed I put a black big liner under my bed sheet in case my waters broke, and it was just as well because when I turned over in bed about half an hour later I felt the familiar 'whoosh'. I was too scared to get out of the bed and call to Craig in case I made a mess on the carpet, so I phoned him from my mobile and he came running upstairs in about three seconds.

Craig called his mum while I got dressed and as soon as she arrived we headed straight to the hospital. I was put on a monitor which confirmed I was contracting, and by that time the pain was really kicking in so I asked for an epidural. It was a very good move.

At about 1.30am I was lying in a bed in the delivery suite and Craig was on a recliner by the side of me. We both started to drift off to sleep but then I was woken up by Craig's snoring. I went to sit up and I felt really strange.

Suddenly all these alarms went off and a doctor and some nurses came rushing in. They put loads of fluid into me because my blood pressure had slowed right down so I was in danger of passing out. Somehow Craig managed to sleep through the whole thing!

Six hours later nothing was happening so the doctor decided to put me on a drip to speed things up. By 9am I was fully dilated but the baby wasn't quite where they wanted her to be so they said they'd leave me to rest for a while. Finally, just after 10am the doctor said he wanted me to start pushing. I only did five sets of three pushes before she popped out. She came into the world on 10th September at 10.41am, weighing 6lbs 10oz. Even though she was still quite light she is still my biggest baby to date.

When we saw her for the first time Craig and I both looked at each other and thought the same thing – 'she's got jet black hair!' Craig was a bit shocked and I laughed and said: 'Don't worry, she is yours babe!'

I stayed in hospital for two nights because I hadn't breast fed for ages and I wanted to make sure everything was going to be okay. To start with she wouldn't latch on at all and we later discovered that she's got tongue-tied, so she's got to have the underneath of her tongue snipped a little bit so that it can come out properly. When I first heard that I was horrified but the doctors assured me that it's a very normal procedure and it's a really common thing in babies.

When we took the new arrival home Craig and I both

took to having a newborn like ducks to water and loved every minute of it, so did Brooke and Tommy. They absolutely adore her. We soon got into a good routine where I do all of the night feeds and Craig looks after her while I take naps during the day. And, of course, the kids love helping out where they can.

Name wise, I'd always really liked Madison, but Craig and I felt like Madison Pearson was a bit of a mouthful so we decided against it. I suggested Miley and Craig loved it straight away so that was an easy decision. We were going to have Faith as her second name but I thought Beau was really pretty, so we ended up having a bit of a stand off about it. Brooke and Craig both wanted Faith but in the end I decided that because I'd gone through the pain of giving birth to her I got to decide! So Beau it is.

We were inundated with presents from people and we felt so spoilt. My living room was like a branch of Interflora and Simon Cowell and his team even sent me some Stella McCartney baby clothes. She's a very lucky little girl.

It was lovely being able to take some time out to bond with Miley but I definitely missed singing. I was almost itching to go back to work after a few weeks. I was so desperate to belt out some songs I even thought about searching out somewhere locally I could go and do karaoke! I'm so lucky because Miley can travel with me a lot when I'm working, and her and Craig and the kids will be coming on some of the tour with me which will be great fun.

Weight-wise, I didn't put on that much during my third pregnancy and once I'd had Miley I was more inclined to get back into shape than I had before, and I still am. I guess I've got an agenda because I've got a tour to do.

When I look back now on everything that happened during and since *The X Factor*, it seems mad to think that I entered it on a whim, but I think people need to make more decisions in that way. We all worry and think about things too much and it holds us back. It's easy to talk yourself out of things. Sometimes you have to ignore the doubts and the negative reasons for not doing something and just go for it.

I've learnt so much about myself over the past year. I've definitely learnt to appreciate my kids more; I have so much more patience with the children and Craig and I talk more than we ever have. We had so many heart-to-hearts during my time on *The X Factor* and we're not scared of upsetting the structure of what keeps us together any more. We endured an incredibly testing time and we came out the other side happier and stronger for it.

My family are what got me through everything and the support I had was unbelievable. If it wasn't for them I would never have been able to achieve the things I have. I feel so lucky to have such amazing people around me.

I've made some brilliant new friends since I was on *The X Factor*. I have to be a bit careful when I'm meeting new people now because I worry that people will want to befriend me for the wrong reasons, but I am pretty good at spotting people who may have an agenda. Obviously it's no secret that I'm massive Leicester City fan and Craig and I have become really pally with some of the players. Conrad Logan and his misses Vicky are going to be godparents to Miley, and we also spend a lot of time with Jamie Vardy and his girlfriend Becky and Gary Taylor-Fletcher and his wife Viv. They're our mates now and I don't think about them being footballers any more because we're all so close. I've also got amazing fans from all over the country and beyond that have fought my corner every step of the way and I'm so grateful to them. I know people always say they wouldn't be anything without their fans but it's true.

I've been asked if I would I go back and do everything the same, all over again. My honest answer? Probably not, simply because of how hard it was being away from my family. If I could go back and do it all again knowing what I know now, then yes, I would, because I would be more prepared for it. I would know what to expect. But I wouldn't want to go blindly into something that massive again. Anyone who wants to do something that's life changing has to accept that it's going to be difficult in some ways. No one ever said changing your life is easy.

The best advice I could give to anyone who was going to enter for *The X Factor* is to make sure you have people around you who will support you, and that you're doing it for the right reasons. Also, grow another layer of skin, because you're going to need it. But most importantly, remember that if you don't try, you'll never know – and you have nothing to lose. If you want something that badly you have to go for it. Like I did, you have to dare to dream.

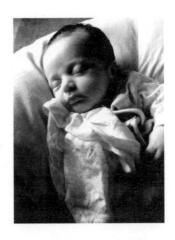

My dear little Miley beau, you were made with such love, you were carried with such care and you entered the world to such proud parents! Mummy, Daddy, Brooke and Tommy love you to the moon and back xx